Women's Education
Harnessing the Gender Power

Women's Education
Harnessing the Gender Power

Dr. Jasprit Kaur Soni

AUTHORSPRESS

Worldwide Circulation through Authorspress Global Network
First Published 2008
by
Authorspress
E-35/103, Jawahar Park
Laxmi Nagar, Delhi-110 092
e-mail: authorspress@yahoo.com

Women's Education: Harnessing the Gender Power
ISBN 978-81-7273-416-9

Printed in India at Tarun Offset, Delhi.

Dedicated

To the Inspiring and Sacred
Memory of My Loving Brother

Late Sardar Amit Singh Bagga

Dedicated

Preface

This book is an effort to analyse the effect of education in the all-round development of women's personality—physical, intellectual, mental and emotional. Has literacy and education helped them to understand the meaning of human rights and human dignity? This book stresses on capacity-building programmes for women to face the emerging challenges in promoting human development in key areas such as literacy, women and child development.

All efforts have been made to ensure the avoidance of errors and to make the work trustworthy. But to err is human, and if any are detected, I tender my apologies. I am sure that in spite of some inherent weaknesses in the work caused by the limitations of the study, the findings of the research will be found to be useful and applicable.

I am deeply indebted to my father Sardar Gurubachan Singh Bagga, my elder sister Dr. Basant Kaur Dua and my elder Brother Dr. Atam Prakash Singh Bagga who always have been a source of inspiration to me.

I am particularly grateful to my in-laws who took great pains and geared me up to undertake this difficult task.

My daughter Miss Anushik Soni (B.E., Information and Technology) deserves affection and special thanks for bearing the hardship during field work and completion of the study.

I must thank my husband Sardar Arvind Singh Soni for not only bearing with me in the difficult times of completing this study, but also for helping me on all counts. Without his cooperation it would not have been possible for me to complete this work.

Lastly, I wish to record my thanks to Authorspress, New Delhi, who undertook the task of publishing this book and completing it in a very short time.

Dr. Jasprit Kaur Soni

List of Tables

List of Graphs

Abbreviations

DPEP	-	District Primary Education Programme
DWCRA	-	Development of Women and Children in Rural Areas
EAS	-	Employment Assurance Scheme
ECCE	-	Early Childhood Care and Education
IGNOU	-	Indira Gandhi National Open University
IOM	-	International Organisation for Migration
IRDP	-	Integrated Rural Development Programme
JRY	-	Jawahar Rojgar Yojana
MLL	-	Minimum Levels of Learning
MNCs.	-	Multi-National Companies
NBT	-	National Book Trust
NCERT	-	National Council of Educational Research and Training
NEEM	-	National Elementary Education Mission
NFE	-	Non-Formal Education
NLM	-	National Literacy Mission
NOS	-	National Open School
NRY	-	Nehru Rojgar Yojana
NSS	-	National Sample Survey
PMRY	-	Prime Minister's Rozgar Yojana
PMUVPEP	-	Prime Minister's Urban Poverty Eradication Programme
PROBE	-	Public Report On Basic Education

POA	-	Progamme Of Action
SIDA	-	Swedish International Development Authority
SSA	-	Sarva Shiksha Abhiyan
TRYSEM	-	Training Rural Youth for Self-Employment
UGC	-	University Grant Commission
UEE	-	Universalisation of Elementary Education
UPE	-	Universalisation of Primary Education
SHGs	-	Self-Help Groups

Contents

1

Introduction
Women's Education: Making a Dormant Volcano Live

Gender bias is worldwide phenomenon, but it is especially pernicious in the Third World, where most of women's activities take place for the purpose of household consumption. With a hue and cry for gender equality, this powerful and perfectionist male image and resulting suppressed emotional needs, has also started targeting women. On one side, women have become more hardworking, educated, loyal, dedicated and responsible; on the other, the dual role of housewives and career women impose a great strain on them.

Despite women's increased percentage in higher education, their greater commitment to politics as a career and equal opportunity legislation, women leaders in every country remain a small fraction of those in higher positions in politics. The leaders are of the opinion that women could never live up to the expectations of the people in taking a country to the heights aspired. Most political parties are reluctant to select women as leaders. Some of the political parties continue to resist the prospect of parting with 33 per cent seats for women in the legislative assemblies and parliament. Only 44 women of the 355 women who contested have been elected in the Lok Sabha elections with the highest number – seven – MPs coming from Uttar Pradesh alone. The highest number of women contestants, 62, were also from Uttar Pradesh from where the Bill is facing resistance from the ruling Samajwadi Party. It's the actions, not the lip service that really matters.

The two main political parties claiming to be champions for women's reservation – the Congress and the BJP—gave the party ticket to 45 and 30 women, respectively. There were as many as 117 women candidates who did not contest under any political banner. The remaining tickets were given by the smaller political parties. "Take measures, including, where appropriate, in electoral systems that encourage political parties to integrate women in elective and non-elective public positions in the same proportion and at the same levels as men; Protect and promote the equal rights of women and men to engage in political activities and to freedom of association, including membership in political parties and trade unions; Review the differential impact of electoral systems on the political representation of women in elected bodies and consider, where appropriate, the adjustment or reform of those systems" the (Beijing Declaration) clearly suggests the magnitude of the problems we are facing cannot be subdued because politicians prefer not to address the problem if they can possibly avoid it. History might eventually reveal that the anti-women attitude is among the greatest threats to sustainable development and the future of humankind.

What we learned from the experiences is that the more you put yourself in a winning position, the more you are likely to win. The higher Self can be a wonderful guide and it will certainly give you the confidence and the platform for the bigger stage. Society is changing rapidly and being a perfect politician is no longer an exclusive male privilege. Women leaders, all over the world, are taking over in a big way. They are no longer content to work in the traditional position of teachers, receptionists and family caretaker. They will have to understand that there is just a small opening for opportunity and it will be closing rather rapidly if they do not grab it; there is not a moment to lose. Political leaders have an important role to play in addressing these challenges. The good news is that political parties seem to be realising that they can no longer ignore these issues.

Women power has been grossly underrated. The women may not be highly qualified but their wisdom cannot be doubted; they may not be physically very strong but their mental strength and readiness to work hard speak volumes about their character;

finally, they may be inhibited leaders but their extraordinary skills and interpersonal abilities cannot be doubted. Women represent a major force, a dormant volcano, a repository of immense potential and abilities. Empowerment of women through education, economic freedom and political leadership can lead to the revolutionary era of development of human resource. Women will feel a sense of belonging towards the people and nation, and this will form the key for the success. Our leaders have to first understand the perceptions, values, beliefs of the people, and when we create awareness in the minds of women and educate them about the same, it will have a great effect. This particular strategy should be used and there is need to educate the people and women about the importance of this issue. For years, women were content with whatever treatment and services they had across to and were offered to them. The advent of media, television in particular, has created awareness in the minds of women. Increasing literacy rate and media penetration have laid the foundation for change in the behaviour of people towards women. The effects of globalisation have finally reached the people of India. The changing face of globalisation has not only transformed the lives of general people, but has also had its effect on the women mindset. Women are no longer the same, they now need more than what they wanted earlier. There is a sea change in the attitudes, lifestyles and preferences of women. This behavioural change in the attitudes of women has indeed forced politician and leaders to give a serious thought about women's issues.

There is a certain ethical know-how to survive and flourish in any situation and environment. It appears that politics in our lives is a fact we all have to live with. We learn the system, and work round it when we can. To be able to determine the requirements of each situation and each person one faces, and to select just the right approach to make things work, and necessarily in a manipulative way, is the nature of a politically savvy person. One must be a friendly and helpful person, good at building relationships. In the process of building relationships, one must make oneself and one's work visible. Being visible is a very important skill and a mark of political savvy. All these contributed to one's getting ahead. One must be politically astute and realistic about the nature of human beings, while at the same time believe in ethics and values. This helps one move upwards without necessarily compromising one's principles. It is possible to put one's career on the fast track by practising positive politics. The one who gets ahead is the one who walks the middle road. The politically astute are skilled at reading the power structures—who the decision-makers are—and then, act upon these.

We must give women opportunity to work at every level when they are consciously making the effort to develop. It is affirmed that humans are born equal, that they are entitled to equality of opportunity, and this principle should be practised. Take the initiative to its logical end and it would "transform" the life of the women. This factor will play a very crucial role and give them a sense of participation. Mary Kay Ash says, "Don't limit yourself. Many people limit themselves to what they think they can do. You can go as far as your mind lets you. What you believe, remember, you can achieve." This is a democratic leap forward that will elevate women's status, which, despite a late start, could finally make it.

The study revealed that parents of high income, small family structure, higher education and occupation at all levels favoured their daughters going to school. "There has been an impressive growth in the area of higher education with an increase in annual student enrolment from 7.26 million in 1997-98 to 9.95 million in 2003-04. Enrolment of women students rose from 2.45 million in 1997-98 to 4.03 million in 2004-05, constituting 40.22 per cent of the total enrolment." Parents of both the schoolgoing girls and dropout girls expressed dissatisfaction towards the prevailing school conditions. The socio-economic conditions are more conclusive to schoolgoing girls than to dropout girls.

Adequate and quality women's education is considered as an essential prerequisite for economic independence of women. It will lead them to improve job knowledge and skills, and will also be helpful in eliminating fear in attempting new tasks. It will help them prepare new, relevant guidelines for work. It is a proven aid in encouraging and achieving self-development and self-confidence; it will boost the morale of women, goodwill and image of women. It will help women in identifying with government's mission, objectives, policies; it will also help in fostering authenticity, openness and trust among women. Education will create the appropriate climate for growth in communication, and provide information on equal opportunity and affirmative action among women. Education will be helpful in providing information to women for future needs of self and society and will provide a good climate for learning, growth and coordination. Education will eliminate suboptimal behaviour in women, and will internalise and operationalise motivational variables of recognition, achievement, growth, responsibility and advancement.

Education is a mission to inspire fresh thinking; it is an encouraging innovative thinking throughout life, and a proactive integrating innovation and innovative thinking into everyday life. Education is a mission in handling conflict, thereby helping to prevent stress and tension; it will also be helpful in developing leadership skill, motivation, loyalty, better attitudes, improved interpersonal skills. It is now time to rethink, reframe and refocus our efforts to ensure that education is indeed integrated throughout all aspects of our lives. Education can no longer be confined to select people. The government and leaders must ensure that support to women are in place to encourage them in broad participation and action.

We are not talking about the typical housemaid who can only wash and clean but with the increasing availability of choices and exposure to the good things of life, women have shortly undergone a drastic change. It is felt that the education imparted to these homes was extremely regressive. If they get specialised training this will play an important part in imparting values in developing the better survival skills against the vagaries of competitive way of life.

Education directed towards human understanding and goodwill, the safeguarding of dignity and freedom, and respect for human dignity. A majority of women prefer to choose or are ordered to choose domestic work over work for market. Rising living standards and poverty reduction across the globe are to a great extent the result of education and technological advances. Voluntary professional organisations of teachers should be treated as partners in educational development. Benjamin Disraeli declared long ago, "Upon the education of the people of this country, the fate of this country depends." Therefore, all progressive countries invest the best of their resources for education. The global education conference at Jomtien, Bangkok, bodly launched EDUCATION FOR ALL IN 1990. These include data collection and monitoring, target setting, the provision of women-friendly working conditions, fair and transparent recruitment procedures, confidence- building and awareness-raising which will be supported through the appropriate training programmes. These qualities can effectively help tackle the seemingly intractable and the most formidable of problems and can influence the government to move in the right direction. The support will go a long way towards enabling to clear the problems in this region, and improve the lives of a large numbers of people. So how do you bring about change, real change?

Women will have to make many adjustments in their life, and will have to do things differently so that they can improve. We genuinely believe that the desired outcomes are difficult but not impossible. We all know it would be a very difficult but their confidence and education will make them see it through. If they just try to stand up and show that they aren't scared or have no fear, they have a chance to prove their worth. Only education can get them this far, and is way up there as well because it opens up a lot of avenues. Once Nelson Mandela said, "Education is the most powerful weapon of change in the world." Education has been the driving force behind many recent developments. Women would be looking for amelioration of the situation which would dispel some of the concerns that they are experiencing today, suppression of the elementary democratic rights of women. This will become a reality if we don't place an unreasonable burden on women. The government must assess and spell out a policy, identify the targets and problem areas and detail a strategy, which will have to be adopted. The government's efforts are being undertaken in a piecemeal and casual manner.

Education will leverage women's skills and knowledge, and make effective use of the latest information technology tools to find better ways to serve their country and the people. It will reorient them as far as the problems of the people and especially women are concerned by adopting a more open approach. Summer Savon says, "It's becoming apparent that female insights such as connection, introspection, intuition and complexity of relationship are more appropriate concepts to describe what we now know about reality." The Constitution of India has given equality of education opportunities irrespective of any type of discrimination including sex. In the post-independent India, it is felt that women's education should be given more importance. It is felt that education of women is essential to achieve the goals of democracy and equality. Women can use knowledge to create sustained competitive advantage, and they will generate their own ideas which would then be developed. Education will also incorporate the ability in women to rescue from "false negatives" and prepare them to serve a cause. Five thrust areas, viz., adult literacy, primary education, decentralisation of management of education and technical education, have been identified to achieve universalisation of the elementary education to make education relevant to the needs of the community, and also to meet new challenges of liberalisation and globalisation of the economy. Had we implemented this programme diligently, we would have by now eliminated illiteracy.

Steps should also be taken to ensure that the sector which is one of the highest generator of employment in the country provides more job opportunities to women. Cheryl F says, "A shared responsibility of women leaders on campus is to make their system more receptive to the presence and progress of women as a group." It is a fact that not much attention is paid to the profile of female teachers, especially about their academic and professional qualifications and competencies to tackle the complexities of today's education.

A quality education can make the difference between success or failure, and revolves around needs and the individual's preferences to have a work-life balance. Quality education has a powerful role to play for converting human beings into human asset. Now, women are considered as an asset instead of a liability and the doors of education are open for women.

WORKS CITED

Beizing Declaration.

Economic Survey, 2005-06.

Social Action, vol. 52, No. 4, Oct.-Dec., 2002.

Miracle of Teaching, Vol. VII, No. 1, Jan-April-2007.

CSR Year Book, 2000.

2

Indian Education at a Glance

Article 26 of the Universal Declaration of Human Rights proclaims that "Everyone has the right to education". To achieve this goal the following principles are laid down:

1. Education shall be free, at least in the elementary and fundamental stages.
2. Technical and professional education shall be made generally available and higher education shall be equally accessible to all, on the basis of merit.
3. Education shall be directed to the full development of the human personality.
4. Education shall be directed to the strengthening of respect for Human Rights and Fundamental Freedoms.
5. Education shall promote understanding, tolerance and friendship among all nations, racial or religions groups.
6. Education shall undertake activities, for the maintenance of peace.
7. Parents have a prior right to choose the kind of education that shall be given to their children.

Education is different from the education imparted today in the universities and colleges, as education is to develop skill and leadership qualities in the students. This can hardly be achieved in the present scenario. The question that immediately comes to mind is: who is going to impart the skill and leadership qualities in the students? Needless to say, it is the teachers and faculty. However, the quality of faculty in colleges and universities in

India is poor, and this calls for quality system in the colleges and universities in India. With winds of change sweeping over the education firmament, students want quality teachers, not authoritative disciplinarians. In fact they may soon act as facilitators rather than conventional teachers, but now they will have to create a scenario of excellence. For this, they will have to display basic personal traits to facilitate an environment of excellence. These basic tools include self-esteem, enthusiasm, humility, a positive attitude, and good communication skills. So if you are equipped with these, you can set off on a journey of excellence.

The fact that large number of different kinds of colleges and universities have been set up during the last few years, makes one wonder as to how these institutions have managed to have competent core faculty, and how they manage to update them. In order to survive and to grow in the present highly competitive and rapidly changing global environment, the expectations of students are on the rise, and educational institutions have to groom students as leaders to meet the challenges by imparting high quality education with an eye on international competition. This means these institutions need to introspect and re-examine the roles of their faculty and fulfilling the expectations of students, and reorient themselves to the task of providing quality education. The development of a nation along with a conscious and productive citizen is dependent upon the standards of education.[1]

Education is not to stuff the child's mind with details and data but to free it from fear and prejudice. In the centenary celebrations speech Mrs. Indira Gandhi called education a liberating, democratising force, cutting across the barriers of caste and class, smoothing out inequalities imposed by birth and other circumstances.[2] Education is widely assumed to be a fundamental prerequisite for participation in the advanced sectors of society. Higher skills, greater information, and knowledge are essential for administration, improvement in productivity, and citizenship in a modern democracy. Great hopes have been pinned on education to bring about social change towards modernisation. Education not only enables an individual to adjust to changes already taking place but it is itself the means whereby he/she can accelerate such changes.[3]

There is need for a change in the mindset of Indian colleges and universities, which do not think beyond awarding degree to students who are able to pay high fees. The changing perspectives in education need to induce a paradigm shift in the vision of the educational institutions and the role of faculty members. Indian colleges and universities need to understand that imparting knowledge on theories and concepts in curriculum and completing laid-down courses through lectures and assignments is not enough. What is required is a paradigm shift in the vision of the colleges and universities and the role and objectives of the faculty. Indian colleges and universities, faculty need to develop the ability to apply knowledge for solving today's practical problems; improve the analytical skills; help students in developing imaginative and innovative solution to deal with real-life situations.

The faculty can develop the skills through several pedagogic tools. To foster quality education in Indian colleges and universities, professional development of faculty members is also the need of the hour, for this change in the culture of colleges and institutions, career and professional development of each and every faculty member is sought. Ethics, education and experience are the integral and essential elements that must be possessed by any quality faculty member. These are important for everyone, but these are especially important for the custodians of future generations vested by the society.

An important point is that we need to develop good quality research through the faculty, which is virtually non-existent in many colleges and universities; if this exists it is only a formality and is of very low quality. Research should be considered as an educational strategy. It will keep students abreast with the latest thinking; it will change the very character of education. Involvement of students, and most importantly the involvement of the faculty members is a must in the research, and quality research and development of new ideas is critical for quality education. If faculty members are not engaged in the research and development of new ideas, they have hardly anything to contribute to students who have all information. If research can provide some learning to the rest of the world, it signifies quality automatically. The faculty members may initiate interdisciplinary research.

Emphasis on field research will help the faculty members enhance their knowledge and will sharpen their mental faculty, infuse confidence and motivate them, thereby improving their overall quality. Exchange programmes through seminars, conferences, workshops and symposiums should become compulsory for students and faculty members.

A good educational management can be successful in the implementation of large scale change in pursuit of quality in this highly competitive era of globalisation. For this there is a need to identify the change and set the vision, define the basic purpose, goals, parameters or requirements of the system. Each one has to adopt a long-term perspective and motivate the elements of the system to surmount the resistance, while managing the transition, irrespective of the designation they have.

Good education can influence the lives of people, and can shape a person's mind and also help to determine that person's destiny forever. Education will help him grow as a humble person and have an opportunity to employ a perspective both creative and effective to leverage and focus the strength of imagination for drawing himself into positive solution and sources, to decipher the constraints and recurrences of his life for gaining access to greater energy and consciousness. Education is an important institution in any modern or modernising society. Historically education has passed practically every sphere of human life. Learning in India, through the ages, was sought not for its own sake, but for the sake and as a part of religion. It was regarded as a means of salvation or self-realisation, as the means to the highest end of life, viz., *mukti* or emancipation. Knowledge of the Self is the one direct means for emancipation. As fire is necessary for cooking, so without knowledge of the Self there can be no emancipation. Action or *karma* cannot destroy ignorance – knowledge does. The Supreme Soul appears finite on account of ignorance. But when that ignorance is destroyed, verily that one Atma or Soul shines by itself like the sun when the clouds are dispelled.[4] It is therefore obvious that ancient Indian education is to be understood as being ultimately the product of Indian theory of knowledge and corresponding scheme of life and values.

The *Upanishads* mentioned three steps of education, namely, "Sravana', i.e., learning to utterance or texts. It was a system of oral tradition. It assumed the form of mantras or sutras by which the maximum meaning was compressed within the minimum of words. 'Mantras' is deliberation or reflection on the topics thought. By 'Nidhidyasana' truth could be realised and attained. This could be asked as the highest stage of meditation. Broadly speaking there were three types of educational institutions, namely, 'Guru Kula', where the student availed himself of the opportunity to accomplish his life and character on the pattern of the idealistic life of his teacher by living in close contact with him. The 'Parishad' (academies) provided the forum where students belonging to the higher order of learning gathered and sought further enlightment through discussion and talks. Organised system of education came into existence more during the Buddhist period. Many educational institutions to teach Pali and Sanskrit for primary and higher education were established. This brought monastic schools into existence. However, later on, the monasteries assumed the form of big vihars for education. Some of them rose to the status of universities, the most notable among them are Nalanda and Takshashila. The monastic colleges were neither sectarian in their outlook nor purely theological in their course of study. The Buddhist universities raised the international standard and attracted students from Korea, China, Tibet and Java.

Education in any field depends on what is happening in the world today. Today major structural changes in industries and occupation have taken place. There is constant demand for new specific and genetic skills in relation of human resource development. Challenges of greater competitiveness, technological change and globalisation are being faced by everybody. New sorts of workplace have emerged. There will be no more jobs for life. All need to switch occupation and career several times in a working life. There is a need for educational institutes to be flexible, responsive and creative. There is competition everywhere and getting the work life balance right is a real task of intelligent educational systems. New ways and skills of information handling have to be resorted. We have to delineate the characteristics of the fluid and changing communities. During the nineteenth century, education became one of the recognised responsibilities of most modern states, what T.H. Marshal has called a 'Social right'.

Even during the British periods efforts were made to give new direction to education by the towering personalities such as Lokmanya Tilak, Sir Sayed Ahmad Khan, Pdt. Madan Mohan Malviya, Rabindranath Tagore, Mahatma Gandhi and Dr. Zakir Hussain. There is greater emphasis on culture, leisure and creativity. Tapping of the new sources of information and knowledge is absolutely necessary for timely management of system. There has been a great deal of accomplishment in the field of education since independence. The learning citizens for the twenty-first century need to be comfortable with own identity, with confidence and self-esteem. High levels of technical skills and competences are needed to be developed. They have to be curious, inquisitive creative, inventive and innovative. The learning citizens for the twenty-first century have to be tolerant of difference, open and accommodative to the experiences of others. A sense of both, self and society, independent and cooperative, has to be imbibed. Skills to shuffle back and forth between ideas, concepts and data, evidence and experience are necessary. Critical and analytical thinking including auto-critique is necessary for effective and sustainable development and growth. Having learned, it is imperative to develop the culture of knowing how to know. All these qualities are required for learners and one has to be a learner, teacher and practitioner at the same time. In such changing times, when 'tension-free society' is the greatest need, empowerment of women through education and training will itself have to be a national strategy for making our country a developed nation in future. W. B. Yeats rightly said that "education is not the filling of a pail but the lighting of a fire." The aim of education is not only imparting of knowledge but it awakens the curiosity, the developments of interests, attitudes, beliefs and values. The interests, attitudes and values promote individual to have self-thinking, introspection and judge himself without which it is not possible to become a responsible member of a democratic society.[5]

The Human Resource Development has been assigned a key role in India's development strategy. The resolution on 'National Policy on Education' adopted in 1986 called for a radical reconstruction of education so that it involved (i) a transformation of the system to relate it more closely to the life of people. (ii) a continuous effort to expand education opportunity (iii) a sustained and intensive effort to raise the quality of education at all stages (iv) an emphasis on the development of science and technology and (v) the cultivation of rural and social values. According to the resolution, the education system must produce young men and women of character and ability committed to national service and development.

Education is an integral part of the country's development process and thus had been accorded a high priority. Concerted efforts during the last years have been tremendous increase in the total number of literates. In 1976, through a Constitutional Amendment, education became the joint responsibility of the centre and the state. Primary education was given an overriding priority in order to realise the goal of universalisation of elementary education. The 'Operation Blackboard' scheme had been formulated with a view to bring about substantial improvement in primary school run by the government, local bodies and recognised aided institutions. There was a provision that the nation, as a whole world, assume the responsibility of providing resource support for implementing programmes of educational transformation, reducing disparities, scientific and technological research and involvement of women and encouragement of female education.

Universalisation of Elementary Education (UEE), education of illiteracy in the age group of 15-35 under the National Literacy Mission (NLM) and development of vocational education are the thrust areas identified in the education sector in the Eighth Plan. Non-Formal Education (NFE) programmes which caters to the needs of dropouts, working children and out of school children has been expanded. Under the revised Eighth Plan in 1993 NFE caters to the states / union territories in the ratio of 60:40 and 90:10 to run the co-educational and girls' centres respectively. With the increase of student strength in elementary schools, the number of schools increased. Universalising access to primary education and improvement of basic school infrastructure must be a core objective of the Tenth Plan. This would mean targeting the provision of one teacher for every group of 40 children for primary and upper primary schools, opening of a primary school / alternate schooling facility within 1 km of every habitation, provision of free textbook to all SCs / STs children and girls at the primary and upper primary school, management and repair of school buildings through school management committees, provision of opportunities for Non-Formal and Alternative Education for out of school children in the most backward areas and for unreached segments of the population in response to local needs and demands articulated at the grassroots level.[6]

The importance of higher education accelerated markedly after independence in 1957. It received a new momentum, and emphasis was laid on the education of the children from the weaker section of society. In spite of limitation, education has been one of the most influential instruments of modernisation in India. After independence, the University Grants Commission was set up in 1953. After the Education Policy of 1968, came the National Education Policy of 1986. this policy lays special emphasis on spreading knowledge, instilling a sense of purpose, to accelerate the process of social change, to develop social consciousness, growth of scientific moral, judicious social values through education, arrangements for vocational education, improving teachers orientation, ethos knowledge and skills and restructuring education system in such a way that a society is built which is based on social, political, and economic justice and equality of opportunity to the Indian citizen.

Today education is considered to be pivotal for social and economic development through development of human resource. This is reflected in the National Policy on Education, 1986 and in the budgetary allocation of resources. The Eighth Plan outlay of education (central and states) at Rs. 19,600 crore is higher than the Seventh Plan expenditure of Rs. 7, 633 crore by 2.6 times. In keeping with this set-up, the Central Plan outlay for education has been substantially increased from Rs. 1,825 crore in 1995-96 to Rs. 3,383 crores in 1996-97. Till the Sixth Plan, education was taken to be a social service rather than an input in the development process. The Ninth Plan outlay for education (centre and states) at Rs. 20, 381.64 crore was higher than the Eighth Plan expenditure of Rs. 7,443 crore by 2.7 times. The Central Plan outlay for education has been substantially increased from Rs. 1,825 crore in 1995-96 to Rs. 5,450 crore in 2000-2001, Rs. 5,920 crore in 2001-2002.

The outlay for elementary education was 64.19 per cent of the total Central Sector Plan outlay in 2001-2002. Further the outlay consisted of Rs. 648 crore for secondary education, Rs. 575 crore for university and higher education, Rs. 120 crore for adult education but adult illiteracy rate remained at 44.2 percent, and Rs. 575 crore for technical education.

There should be an increase in literacy rate to 75 per cent within the Plan period.[7] According to the 2001 Census, the literacy rate is 64.8 per cent. The highest literacy rate of 90.92 per cent is in Kerala and the lowest literacy rate of 47.53 per cent is in Bihar. The literacy rates among men and women are 75.20 per cent and 53. 6 per cent respectively.

The Indian Constitution specifies the attainment of universal elementary education among the directive principles of state policy. The objective has not yet been achieved and that nearly half of India's population remains illiterate. Even more disconcerting is the fact that literacy rate and education levels among the disadvantaged groups (women, Scheduled Castes, Tribes, religious minorities) remain much below that of the rest of the population. Corrective actions will, of course, require massive increase in public outlay to expand and improve school facilities, appoint adequate teachers, strengthen incentives for enrolment and have greater involvement of the local community and in decision making body. The only possibility appears to be a national effort in which the community, teachers, planners and policy makers take a lead, and the government and other agencies take a supporting role. Further delay would only shift the target to a more distant future.

Literacy: Literacy of males in India is 67 per cent as compared to 82 per cent of the world figure, and for females in India the adult literacy rate is 39 per cent as compared to 67 per cent of the whole world.[8] According to the Population Commission of United Nations the ability to both read and write a simple message with understanding in any language is a sufficient basis for classifying a person as literate. The Indian Census has adopted this definition.

Ever since independence, elimination of illiteracy has been one of the major concerns of the government. However, in view of country's vast size, huge population and limited resource position, not much progress could be made in this direction. Thus even in 1991, the literacy rate for the country, as a whole, was as low as 52.21 per cent. However literacy recorded an increase by 8.65 per cent as the figure in 1981 was 43.56 per cent. The following table shows the literacy rate for male female and total population since 1901 and for the state and union territories

Literacy rate: Literacy rate is the number of literate persons for each hundred people and expressed in percentage.

Table 2.1

Indian Literacy Rate

Year	*Persons*	*Males*	*Females*
1901	5.3	9.8	0.6
1911	5.9	10.6	1.1
1921	7.2	12.2	1.8
1931	9.5	15.6	2.9
1941	16.1	24.9	7.3
1951	16.7	25.0	7.9
1961	24.0	34.4	12.9
1971	29.5	39.5	18.7
1981	36.2	46.9	24.8
1991	52.2	64.13	39.29
2001	64.8	75.2	53.6

Even though the Indian education scenario, over the past few decades, has been characterised by massive quantitative expansion at all levels, it is still faced with a staggering backlog of high literacy levels of over 47 per cent in 1991. The attainment of the goal of universal elementary education still remains a distant possibility. Concentrated efforts have, therefore, to be made to wipe off illiteracy in the shortest possible time if the country has to take rapid strides in its socio-economic development. With this in view, several schemes and projects have been taken up to eradicate illiteracy and promote education among the masses. The male-female literacy gap, which was to the tune of 25 per cent in the 1991 census, has been reduced to around 20 per cent in 2001. Education backwardness is a major reason for the women lagging behind. Of the world's one billion illiterate adults, two-thirds are women. Two-third of the 150 million children worldwide who are not in schools are girls.[9]

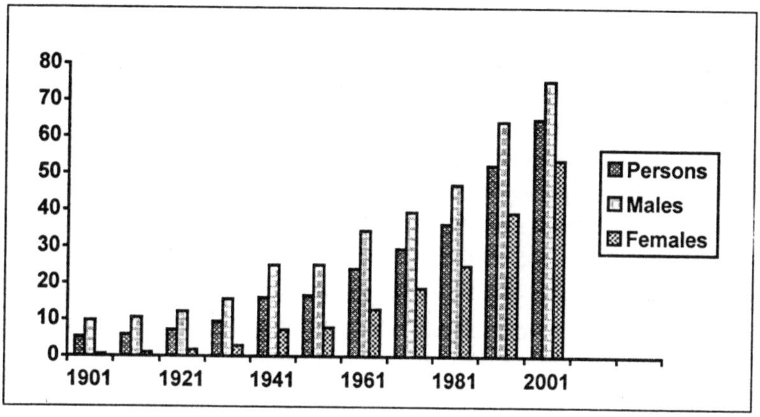

Graph 2.1 : Indian Literacy Rate

The highest priority is accorded to the programme of universalisation of elementary education for fulfilment of the constitution directive for providing free and compulsory education to all children upto the age of 14. The revised programme of action, 1992 of the National Policy on Education 1986 resolved to achieve this goal before we enter the twenty-first century. A National Elementary Education Mission (NEEM) was set up on 30 April 1995 to implement the programme in mission mode.

Education is free up to lower secondary stage in many states and union territories and free up to higher secondary level in some states. The adoption of 10 +2 +3 pattern was first recommended by the Calcutta University Commission in 1917-1919. It transfers the intermediate stage from university to school where it really belongs; 28 states and 7 union territories follow the 10 + 2 pattern.

The Constitution (Eighty-Third Amendment) Bill, 1997 was introduced in the Rajya Sabha on 28 July 1997 to make right to free and compulsory education for children from 6 to 14 years of age a Fundamental Right. The Parliamentary Standing Committee on HRD proposed some modification in the Amendment Bill. Accordingly a revised Draft Constitution Amendment Bill is under consideration of the government.

The situation of women education in India is far below satisfaction. In 1946-47, for every 100 literate boys 33 girls were literate. The 1971 census showed that 39.5 per cent of the males and 18.7 per cent of female were literate in the country which increased to 24.88 per cent in 1981. The enrolment of girls as a ratio of total enrolment during 1992-93 was 43 per cent at the primary stage, 18 per cent at other below degree stage and 33 per cent at the higher education stage.[10]

Our performance in the field of education is one of the most disappointing aspects of our developmental strategy. Out of approximately 200 million children in the age group 6-14 years, only 120 million are in schools and the net attendance in the primary level is only 66 per cent of enrolment. This is completely unacceptable and the Tenth Plan should aim at a radical transformation in this situation. Education for all must be one of the primary objectives of the Tenth Plan. The Sarva Shiksha Abhiyan, which has been launched to achieve this objective, indicates a strong reiteration of the country's resolve to give the highest priority to achieve this goal during the Plan period. It should also be our resolve that the processes of integrating our educational system with the economic needs of the people and of the nation must begin at the primary school stage itself. The objective of education is the total development of a child's personality, in which, character building and physical education, including sports, are crucial ingredients. Assertion of the dignity of labour and vocationalsation of curricula are essential to ensure that a disjunction does not take place between the educational system and the workplace.[11] Based on the recommendations of the National Committee of State Education Mission, a new scheme, Sarva Shiksha Abhiyan (SSA), has been evolved to pursue universal elementary education in a mission mode. The goals of SSA are: all 6-14 age children (i) are in school/ EGS centre/bridge course by 2003, (ii) complete five year primary education by 2007, and (iii) complete eight years of schooling by 2010.

Higher education is imparted through more than 300 universities; out of them 100 are said to be deemed universities and over 12,000 colleges and institutions of higher education in India are affiliated to them. Enrolment of students in universities and colleges has touched the figure of one crore and more than four lakh teachers are employed in these institutions. Among these are 12 central universities and the remaining are functioning under the State Acts. Besides, there are 34 institutions declared as deemed to be universities. The University Grant Commission, set up in 1956, promotes and coordinates university education, and determines and maintains standards of teaching, examination and research in the universities. In higher education, due cognisance has to be taken of the fact that the country has an existing infrastructure which, despite its problems, is still one of the best in the developing world. The country needs to capitalise on this advantage to enhance our competitiveness in the global world.

A quite different approach that also relies on socio-economic theories regards higher education as playing an integral part in schooling's complicity in the reproduction over the generation of an unequal and hierarchical social and sexual division of labour. Women in higher education are found in restricted numbers and in limited subject fields because this is what capitalist society expects, even 'needs'.[12]

Higher education these days demands Quality Assurance (QA). There is a need for a value-frame for direction to assess higher education institutions in India, the need for dissemination and adopting best practices, the role of students in bringing QA in higher education in India. The Government instituted in 1949 a system of National Professorship to honour distinguished academicians and scholars in recognition of their valuable contribution to knowledge. The Indian Council of Historical Research, New Delhi, was set up in 1972 which enunciates and implements a national policy of historical research and encourages scientific writing of history. The Indian Council of Social Science Research, New Delhi, was set up to promote and coordinate Social Science Research in the country. The Indian Council of Philosophical Research with offices at New Delhi and Lucknow review the progress of research in philosophy from time to time. The Indian Institute of Advanced Study, Simla, set up in 1965, is a residential centre for advanced research in the humanities, social science and natural sciences.

The Government of India, Department of Education, has been running, since 1979-80, a programme of Non-Formal Education (NFE) for children of 6-14 age group who remain outside the formal system due to various reasons. Currently 2.97 lakh NFE centres have been sanctioned catering to about 74.25 lakh children. Of the total number of centres about 1.17 lakh centres are exclusively for girls. About 28,788 centres are run by 816 voluntary agencies. The District Primary Education Programme (DPEP) was launched in 1994 as a major initiative to achieve the objective of Universalisation of Primary Education (UPE).

Technical manpower is the main need of the country. The number of degree level institutions are 1.058. Facilities for post-graduate studies and research work (PhD) level have also been created.

Lok Jumbish (People's movement for Education for all) an innovative project with assistance from Swedish International Development Authority has been undertaken in Rajasthan. The basic objective of the project is to achieve 'Education for All' through people's mobilisation and their participation.

The National Open School (NOS) established as an autonomous registered society under the Ministry of Human Resource Development in November 1989 is vested with the authority to examine and certify students registered with it, up to pre-degree level courses. NOS provides opportunities for continuing education to interested learners through its foundation, secondary and senior secondary courses.

The Indira Gandhi National Open University (IGNOU) was established under an Act of Parliament, 1985. Its major objectives are provision of opportunities of higher education to larger segments of the population, introduction of special groups of higher education for specific sections like women and people living in backward regions and hilly areas. The instructional system designed by the university involves a multimedia learning packages. The electronic media components include audio and video cassettes. The total number of students registered for various programmes of study in the IGNOU during 2002 is over 2.98 lakh.

The university has established an extensive student support services network consisting of 46 region centres and 765 study centres situated in different parts of the country. On 26 January, 2001, the "Gyandarshan" channel was launched. Distance education is a mean to bring education to the masses, but if imparted without QA measures in place, it can be a big problem. Therefore, for anyone associated with higher education, a sense of dedication is absolutely vital.

The National Council of Educational Research and Training(NCERT) was set-up in 1981. Major achievements of NCERT were directed towards Early Childhood Care and Education (ECCE). Universalisation of Elementary Education (UEE), Minimum Levels of Learning (MLL), orientation of content and process of education at the school stage, improvement of science education in school, computer literacy, vocationalisation of education, teacher education, utilisation of educational technology, national talent search scholarship and publication of text-book for CBSE affiliated schools in the country. There are eight regional institutes under NCERT.

The National Policy of Education, 1986 envisaged setting up of model schools one in each district of the country. Navodya Vidyalayas are fully residential co-educational institutions providing education up to senior secondary stage. The scheme started with two experimental schools in 1985-86 and has now grown to 446 schools covering as many districts in 33 States/UTs with over 1.27 lakh students on rolls. About 30,000 new students are admitted every year.

The Government of India approved the scheme of Kendriya Vidyalaya Sangathan in 1962 on the recommendation of the Second Pay Commission. Initially, 20 regimental schools in different states were taken over as Central Schools. In 1965, an autonomous body called Kendriya Vidyalaya Sangathan was established with the primary objective of setting up and monitoring Kendriya Vidyalayas to cater to the education needs of the children of the transferable central government employees including defence personnel by providing a common programme of education. At present there are 874 Kendriya Vidyalayas out of which one each is in Kathmandu and Moscow. All Kendriya Vidalayas follow a uniform syllabus.

The National Book Trust (NBT), an autonomous organisation set-up in 1957, functions with the objective of fostering book-mindedness among the people, and providing good reading material for various age groups at moderate prices. The Trust Organises books fairs. The Indian Copyright Act, 1957, was further amended in 1994 in order to check the problem of widespread piracy in the country. The policy of the government is to encourage the development of all the Indian languages including classical, modern and tribal. Through the Kendriya Hindi Sansthan, Agra, the government promotes the development of improved methodology for teaching Hindi to non-Hindi speaking students. Under the schemes for the development of modern Indian languages, the government gives financial assistance to voluntary organisations for bringing out publications like encyclopaedias, dictionaries, books of knowledge and scientific interests. Since 1989, the Trust has been promoting the celebration of National Book Week (14-15 November) on an all-India scale. In 1999-2000 NBT organised book festivals at Barelly and Shillong, the National Book Fair at Bhopal and Chandigarh. For the first time the Trust celebrated the World Book and Copyright Day on 23 April, 1999 in celebration with the Federation of Indian Publishing. In 2000-01, NBT organised book fairs and exhibition at Shimla, Jalandhar, Bilaspur and Brahamapur, and the National Book Fair at Mumbai; 338 Pustak Parikramas were organised through its mobile exhibition vans.

The NCERT is providing assistance to the Department of Education implementing the District Primary Projects (DPEPs) to fulfil the Education for All (EFA). The major project handled by NCERT is the sixth All India Educational Survey conducted in collaboration with the National Information Centre.

Education of Scheduled Caste and Schedule Tribes 1990-91 was the centenary year of Dr. Ambedkar. The National Committee which was set-up under the chairmanship of the then Prime Minister decided that the programme for the development of SCs and STs would continue for the year 1996-97. The programme includes panel discussion, seminars, essay competition, publication of Dr. Ambedkar's biography and his anthology.

The revised Programme Of Action (POA) 1992 is prepared in pursuance of the modified National Policy on Education(NPE). 1986. It provides for continuance of the excisting education programmes for SCs and STs with stress on improving literacy, increasing enrolment and reducing dropout rates among SCs/ STs. The two new schemes under POA launched during the year 1993-94 were Area Intensive Program of Educational Backward Minorities and Financial Assistance for Modernisation of Madarasa Education. The Indian Institute of Technology operates a scheme under which candidates belonging to SCs and STs who fail in the joint entrance examination by a slender margin of marks are given further training and admitted to relevant courses.

A centrally- sponsored scheme, Environmental Orientation to School Education was initiated in 1988-89. The Scheme envisages assistance to voluntary agencies for conduct of experimental and innovative programs aimed at promoting integration of educational program in schools with local environmental conditions.

Important Educational Programmes

National Council of Education Research and Training

Established in 1961, the NCERT acts as the principal agency for academic advice to the Ministry of Human Resource Development, in matters pertaining to the formulation and implementation of policies and programmes for the qualitative improvement of school education. It is mainly engaged in research, development, training and extension, and has provided support to the implementation of the 10+2+3 pattern of education. Besides developing curricula for the various stages of school education, it also produces textbooks in allmost all the subjects for the entire school stage (class I to XII).

District Primary Education Programme

The District Primary Education Programme (DPEP) was launched in 1994 as a major initiative to achieve the objectives of Universalisation of Primary Education (UPE). The programme takes a holistic view of primary education development, and seeks to operationalise the strategy of UPE through district specific planning with emphasis on decentralised management, participatory processes, empowerment and capacity building at all levels. The programme is implemented through the state level registered societies. The programmes aims at providing access to primary education for all children, reducing primary dropout rates to less than 10 per cent, increasing learning achievement of primary school students by 25 per cent, and reducing the gender and social gap to less than five per cent.

Operation Blackboard

In pursuit of the goal of universalisation of elementary education, the 'Operation Blackboard' scheme has been formulated with a view to bringing about substantial improvement in primary schools run by the government, local bodies and recognised aided institutions. The Operation Blackboard scheme, launched in 1987-88, aims at providing essential facilities (two teachers and teaching learning equipment) in all primary schools in the country in a phased manner. The scheme was expanded during 1993-94 to provide a third teacher to primary schools with enrolment exceeding 100 and to cover upper primary schools through provision of additional teachers and teaching learning equipments. The scheme provides 100 per cent central assistance for teaching learning equipment and for salaries of teachers during the plan period; construction of school buildings is states' responsibility. The Operation Blackboard scheme has three components, viz.,

i) provision of at least two all-weather rooms,
ii) provision of at least two teachers, one of them preferably a woman, in every single teacher primary school, and
iii) provision of essential teaching and learning material including blackboards, maps, charts, a small library, toys, games, sports material and some equipment for work experience. It was proposed to implement the scheme of Operation Blackboard in a phased manner covering all the primary schools by the end of the year 1990.

Lok Jumbish

An innovative project called Lok Jumbish (People's movement for education for all) with assistance from the Swedish International

Development Authority (SIDA) has been undertaken in Rajasthan. The basic objective of the project is to achieve, "Education for All" through people's mobilisation and their participation.

The National Programme of Nutritional Support to Primary Education: A National Programme of Nutritional Support to Primary Education commonly called the Midday Meals Scheme launched on 15 August 1995 is aimed at improving enrolment attendance and retention while simultaneously impacting on the nutrition status of students in primary classes.

Mahila Samakhya

The Mahila Samakhya Programme (education for women's quality), launched in 1989 is a women's empowerment project which aims at creating an environment for women to seek knowledge and information with a view to bringing about a change in the perception about themselves and that of the society.

The National Policy on Education, which was approved by Parliament in 1986, seeks to establish, foe the first time in free India's history, a National System of Education, which lays down an overall curricular framework and a core curriculum to establish capability of competence at the end of various stages of education all over the country, reinforce the integrative aspect of society and culture and also establish a value system necessary for an egalitarian, democratic and secular society. The new policy presents the problem of socio-cultural inequalities in a very sharp focus and lists the specific steps in such detail that it could be described as nothing less than a charter, not only for quality of access to education, but also for equalisation with regard to the status of disadvantaged sections of society.[13]

References

1. *Miracle of Teaching*, 03, 2006, p. 103.
2. *Social Action*, vol. 52, No. 4, Oct.-Dec., 2002, p.366.
3. Uttam Kumar Singh, *Women's Education*, Commonwealth Publishers, New Delhi, 1997, p. 261.
4. Adi Sankara, *Atma Bodha* 2-4.
5. *Indian Education Commission Report, 1964-1966.*
6. *Approach Paper to the Tenth Five Year Plan (2002-2007)*, Planning Commission, Government of India, New Delhi, September, 2001, pp. 36-38.

7. Ibid., p. 3.
8. *World Development Report, 1999-2000,* Oxford University Press.
9. Valsamma Antony, 'Empowering the Urban Women through Micro – Enterprises: A Case Study', *The Economic Challenger*, No. 7, Issue 27, April-June, 2005, p.67.
10. *Miracle of Teaching*, op. cit., p. 87.
11. *Approach Paper to the Tenth Five Year Plan (2002-2007)*, op. cit.
12. Uttam Kumar Singh, op. cit., p. 218.
13. CSR, *Year Book*, p. 632.

3

Indian Women at a Glance

Barring the early Aryan period when the women enjoyed due respect and status, they have undergone a steady deterioration in their social status. Subsequent periods impaired their identity and relegated them to an inferior, inhuman and loathsome place in society. Their rights were usurped. They were deprived of education and freedom. Continuous invasions shattered the political structure and casual great upheaveals in the social conditions of the country. Women suffered the most. They came to be regarded as man's shoes. "Manu" carved out a nightmarish horror of his own rhapsody. He usurped their smiles, crushed their dreams and made them an erotic delight for men's lascivious eyes. Their charm and beauty became their worst enemies. He made them a puppet and a silent endurer of men's whims and caprices and pleasure. When a girl-child was born, it came to be considered as inauspicious and unworthy of any celebration or happiness. He equated women with she-wolves or serpents. They were suppressed, oppressed, decimated and regarded as inferior to men. They were confined to the four walls of the home and reduced to be merely another intoxicant (a sex object) like wine and wealth.

Millions of women are victims of the mindset of men who believe that they are 'kings of their cattle' and women their servants. We might not know their names, their stories might never be told. No poems will be written about them and no monuments will be erected to honour their memories but they changed the course of history including contributing significantly to the freedom movement of our country.

Leaders of various religious groups failed to do any justice to women. Islamic Shariat allowed polygamy and equated the evidence of two women with that of one man. Jogi Gorakh Nath called woman a she wolf and the Jains considered women ineligible for *moksha*. Buddhism really allowed the entry of women to the Sanghas. Shakespeare said, "Woman, the name is frailty". Chesterfield considered them as an "agreeable blunder". Tulsidas classified women with cattle, shudras and the vulgar. He portrayed the woman in his couplets as a seductress. Chastity, virginity and purdah were made mandatory for women to block all roads to their liberation. Even world-famous philosopher Socrates said, "The courage of a man and that of woman are not the same. The courage of a man is shown in commanding and that of woman in obeying." Aristotle said, "Woman is an unfinished man, left standing at the lower step in the scale of development. The man is by nature superior and female inferior. The one is the ruler and the other ruled. Woman is weak of will and, therefore, incapable of independence of character or position." Even Christianity did not accord religious equality to women.

The position of women in India is indeed precarious. Child marriage and female infanticide is widespread. Polygamy is freely practised. Widows are forced to observe 'Sati'. Women were taken as slaves by invaders and sold as cattle in foreign markets. 'Purdah' is mandatory for women. There is a need to rehabilitate them to a place of honour. It is asserted by many great personalities that men and women share the grace of God equally and are responsible for their deeds before Him. They repudiated the notion that the women are inherently evil and unclean. They believed that social structure would remain weak and incomplete without the participation of women in social and religious activities. According to them, the role of mother gave women a unique status. They degraded the prevailing values downgrading women, Sikhism, the most modern religion, has proved itself the mouthpiece of women's emancipation. Guru Nanak Dev in Asa-di-Var asks, "Why call her inferior from whom kings are born?" He raised the status of women to a high pedestal and gave them all rights equal to men. Bhai Gurdas defined Sikh's attitude towards women, "Women is one half of the complete personality of man and is entitled to share, secular and spiritual knowledge equality."

Women have also played a stellar role in the liberation of the motherland. Their deeds of valour, self-sacrifice and courage are too many to be recounted. They suffered and sacrificed their lives, and volumes can be written about the glory of women in history. Today many women have distinguished themselves in various challenging spheres as eminent lawyers, doctors, engineers, diplomats, administrators, judges, businesswomen etc.

Women are not helpless; they must never regard themselves as weaker than men. They should not, therefore, beg for men's mercy, nor depend on them. They are not only equal to men but are more than equal to them. They have proved their mettle in whatever field they have chosen to serve. They have stood shoulder to shoulder with men in war and in peace, religious, social, political and in all other walks of life. Every chapter of Indian history is full of their matchless sacrifice and deeds of valour and virtue.

With the rise of democracy, the movement for the emancipation of women gained ground all the world over. In some Western countries women are more emancipated and enjoy much more rights than in India. But still, everywhere, even in the most advanced countries of the world, they suffer from a number of disabilities and are regarded as socially inferior to man. It is a manmade society and man continues to dominate and exploit women. However, such an irrational treatment was a matter of deep concern for the world all over when everyone accept the true fact that man is incomplete without woman. To focus attention on the problem concerning women all the world over, the Decade 1975-86, was declared the International Women's Decade. In the same spirit, 2001-2002 was dedicated to "Women Empowerment".

Time and time again, great personalities have tried to give women their right place which they deserved so well. It is well said, "Educate a man and you educate an individual; educate a woman and you educate a family." The year 2001-2002 dedicated to "Women Empowerment" stressed on seeking meaningful equality in social rights, elimination of discrimination in employment and universal education of women, the lack of which tends to perpetuate the unequal status quo. There is need for improving the condition of women in the weakest sector—the rural, slum and tribal population. The women of India played a silent, a self-effecting role to sustain Indian civilisation down the ages. For their greater participation in national life, it is necessary that they should occupy positions at the decision-making and planning level. A general awakening to the hardship and problems of women has already been created and as a result legal laws have been made more stringent to prevent crimes against women. Since 1947 each Five Year Plan has carefully provided for the health, education, employment and welfare of women. More importantly, planners have been alert and dynamic in defining plan obligation to fit in with changing times. The emphasis is on providing women with 'welfare' and protection. The education of girls should receive emphasis not only on grounds of social justice, but also because use it accelerates social transformations.[1] Our Constitution has given equal rights to women, and no distinction has been made on the basis of caste, religion or sex. The place of women in free India is becoming more and more secure with the change of times. She can no longer be dominated and driven like dumb cattle by man.

Besides all such external factors, the women empowerment comes from within. It is not the external show of fashion, beauty, position or paper qualification—all of which are "skin deep" and will be lost in the event of a scar or a wrinkle. Certainly they are falsely impressive. True power comes from knowing in your heart of hearts that you are good, that you are comfortable with who you are, with your true self. In such a position, a woman would not be easily influenced by other people's opinion of them. "You have got to be your own woman", compatible with yourself, respect yourself and certainly see the positive side of who you really are. Love yourself. It is only when one learns to love the self unconditionally, that it is possible to become truly successful in the outer world of relationships, activities and roles. The inner spiritual awareness and growth is also the key to outer liberation in terms of capacity to survive and thrive in the wider world.

Our educated women's responsibility is tremendous. Women have a significant role in shaping the behaviour and mental make-up of the younger generation. She has the primary duty of returning and shaping the children, the leaders of tomorrow. Woman who was given a prominent role in the family set up, by our heritage and culture today in the modern age, has an important part to play in the national development at large. Swami Vivekananda said, "If you want the nation to prosper include women in every aspect of our life." In a male-dominated society, a woman could rise to the challenge, reclaim her self-respect, live in dignity and accept her very own "specialness". She will no longer need to live up to the male species expectations of her. She could be her own woman and lead the life she wants with the freedom, to do as she pleases. She may no longer need to depend heavily on material things for her crutches or tools in achieving the desires. If only she would listen to her own conscience, to their voice in her heart, she would be able to have herself out of the bowels of such injustice. It is the woman who gives birth to the child, rears the child, creating citizens out of them. So how can she be ignored? If woman is ignored and not educated enough then how is our country going to progress? We have to focus on education and empowerment of women in rural areas, particularly those from socially and economically marginalised groups. It is necessary to bring about a change in women's perceptions about themselves and that of the society in regard to women's traditional roles.

It is necessary to create an environment for women to seek knowledge and information in order to make informed choice at the own pace. It deals exclusively with the quality improvement of women's lives emphasizing on processes and inventions responding to the needs of women and girls. We have to evolve educational institutions which cater exclusively to marginalised girls, particularly in socially backward and underprivileged groups which address the educational needs of adolescent girls, working girls and dropouts. Gender specific pedagogy and teaching–learning materials have to be developed in such cases. Impressive achievements and innovative approaches and efforts by both governmental and non-governmental agencies have led to progress in education in terms of access, enrolment, retention and quality in women education. However, providing access of girls children in schools in difficult circumstances poses a challenge of planning and providing quality education for all. Our colleges, particularly women's colleges, have to be part of such activities.

Demand for Women's Education

In fact the status of women in society is the indicator of a national overall development. Swami Vivekananda said that there is no hope of rise for that family or country where there is no esteem for women, where they live in sadness. For this reason they have to be raised first. This can only be possible by educating them because education improves the earning potential and productivity of women and helps them in organising for asserting their rights. There has been perceptible change in the political, economic and social status of women in the last 50 years, but we cannot claim that the progress is all that satisfactory. Although a little more than half the country's adult population as a whole (52.2%) is now counted as literate, 67.83 per cent of its female population remains illiterate. The wide gap between male and female literacy rates persists at the national level despite spectacular improvements in a few states, led by Kerala.

With education at the crossroads through the world, how can we ignore the problem concerning the access of girls and women to education?[2] Women's education will sensitise women to their rights, raise their levels or aspirations and achievements.[3] The integral development of the nation naturally includes modernisation, urbanisation and industrialisation. Technical knowledge, cultural development and economic progress all are associated with these. Educated women are really empowered to contribute significantly in these fields. In the agricultural field, women participate to a greater extent – but they remain as invisible contributors. An educated woman who has specialised in these areas can render a great service. Women's development is directly related to national development. In the Sixth Five Year Plan a special chapter has been added : "Women's Development". In this it has been mentioned that the strategy should be threefold, i.e., Education, Employment and Health. They are interdependent and dependent on the total development process. The planning commission has defined three major fields for women's development, i.e., Education, Health and Welfare. Education has been continued emphasis in incoming all plans. Education is base of all basics of development process. So everything depends upon the application of education and simple training for improving women's health condition. The pace of women's education will help to be accelerated so that women also become aware of their rights.

There are several things to be done by women in the health and hygiene field. By nature women have the ability to care – to smoothen the suffering. With a professional knowledge of hygiene and contagious disease, they can certainly go a long way in building up a health community. Women can easily save the younger generation from the deadly practices of smoking, drinking and drug abuse. All these activities are now taken by women staying behind the curtain – as a silent catalyst; this is not enough. More proactive steps from individuals and institutions are necessary. There are ever so many openings for young women graduates to serve the nation. Besides contributing to the academic, scientific and technological development, a number of other areas are open and friendly to educated women forestation and food processing are is creating an eco-friendly environment, in this age of acute unemployment, all these from important components of national development.

In every sphere of life the position of women is not satisfactory. Women are mostly engaged in least paid jobs, they work for long hours, bear full responsibility of the home, fetch fuel and water, cook in family production units, bring up children and take care of the sick and aged, without being paid for their labour. This is the stark reality of millions of women. Empowering women indirectly leads to a growing demand for education for girls and enhancing their participation in informal and alternative education system.

In olden days women had to walk miles and miles to bring drinking water and firewood. But the educated woman of today is blessed with LPG gas and microwave oven. Yet we have to bear in mind that even now in rural remote villages there are lakhs of women struggling for basic amenities like this. The International Decade (1975-85) of Women provided an opportunity to scholars for making conscious endeavours to understand the specific problems of women. The literate woman should be quite conscious of energy conservation and eco-friendly practices. Besides contributing to increased production, women can help extensively in preserving food and energy. Above all, as an entrepreneur, she can start her own industry with the technical know-how she has earned, thus contributing to the family income and national income through jobs like fashion designing, tailoring, food processing, poultry farming, flower production, preparing spices and so on. You have multifarious activities pertaining to the women's world. When the power and skill of our women are directed to such creative activities, they would be active partners in national building.

The first step in national development is to recognise their merit and their contribution. Women should really feel proud of their accomplishments and status in the society. But still there is a lot to do to uplift the women. Education is the first step that can open the doors to a much wider world of knowledge and information which were not accessible to women. It will expand opportunities for them, will equip them with more information, will empower them to resist oppression, will enable them to claim their rights and will strengthen them to fight against the social evils and all types of violence against women. God has made all human beings as equal individuals and women have qualities and talent of their own. In India, the position of women in society was supposed to be improved due to the constitutional provision of equal rights for both men and women. But constitutional sanction of political equality of women with men is enjoyed only to a limited extent by the women. Swami Vivekananda said, "There is no chance of welfare of world unless the condition of women is improved. It is not possible for a bird to fly with only one wing."

Women were never designed to be subject to man. She was created to complement his existence. Much work remains to be done to ensure the emancipation of the women. We can never say, we have realised the objectives if we do not achieve this goal of women empowerment which forms the central element for renewal of free India. Let us as men and women take up this call. Let us examine in our struggle for gender and racial equality, where we are so that we may take firm steps together to arrive at where we need to be: a beautiful world for all who live in it. Let us take the analogy of a seed in the soil. Just like we need to till the soil and sow the seed in a suitable climate for a healthy crop, even if we have sown the best of seeds, we need to prepare a fertile ground for the long life and growth of the talented women in every sphere of life.

Tribal Women: Emerging New Elite

Article 15 of the Constitution says, "The state shall not discriminate against any citizen on the ground of religion, race, caste, sex, place of birth or any of them". Article 14 guarantees women equality before law. Articles 16 (1) and (2) provide equal opportunity in employment or appointment to any office under the state.

To be an equal partner in the national development, the women of India should be provided with the facilities of education, employment and health. This can be achieved only by the strong will of the government to implement the various legislatures relating to these basics of the overall development. Our progress on social and economic fronts will not be achieved if we leave tribals especially tribal women, from the mainstream. Despite the law, we are not able to give equal deal to our women, mainly tribal women.

According to the 1991 Census in the field of women's education there is some progress as compared to 1981 census: 15.5 percent women were more literate and percentage of tribal women was doubled but still they were less than half of the percentage of educated males. Among women, Rajasthan has the lowest literacy rate which comes to 20 per cent. In rural areas 11.6 per cent of males are literate. When it comes to the tribal women education it is more dismaying because only 4 per cent among them are literate. In Rajasthan, the state of women's education is further dismaying. The education in general percentage of men's education is two and half times more than literate women. The percentage of tribal men's education is eight time more than that of tribal women. When we compare these figures with the 1981 Census this gives us some consolation—that there is more progress in this field.

The capabilities of tribal women can be expanded by giving them education and make them literate. Education will enhance their ability to participate and contribute to the process of development. PROBE (Public Report On Basic Education) in its findings shows that 57 per cent of girls in the age group of 6 to 14 in rural areas were enrolled in schools. But when we see how many of these girls actually attended the school, this could be dismaying. To make tribals and tribal women more literate, more facilities should be provided, and the infrastructure should be in consonance with the geographical, economical and social conditions.

The tribal women have now started to read and write. Their speed is no doubt very slow, but the tribals now realise the importance of education. The government provides all facilities to them for free education.

One of the main objectives of education planning in our country has been to improve tribal women literacy by accelerating the process of educational development through larger investment and various incentives.

The problem of education among tribal women is definitely not simple. At this critical juncture every tribal girl-child is required to be given the full benefit of educational opportunities for which priority action plan at national level, regional level, state level and district level are required to be immediately adopted without further loss of time.

It is essential to attract the tribal girl students and retain them either in the formal school system or non-formal education (N.F.E.) system and also to check dropout rates. More emphasis has to be laid on elementary education. There is a need to open a good number of residential schools for tribal girls in particular in all the pockets of tribal habitation. There is a need to upgrade such primary schools also. Special vocational education is to impart to tribal girls in crafts like tailoring-cutting, typewriting, embroidery and other non-traditional skills.

Need of the Day

The problem of women's education can be conceptualised as a moral one. The study of women's education is our major concern and we must take it very seriously. The National Policy on Education document made a strong commitment to a well conceived edge in favour of women as an act of faith and social engineering. However, the men outnumber women in India. Most of the women are suppressed and face discrimination within the family where they are told to eat last and least. Still today, in many villages, girls are not allowed to go for further studies in nearby cities, and are not free to talk to menfolk; they remain confined to their home. Literacy is the first step towards acquiring other tools of learning, and can open the doors to a much wider world of knowledge and information than would otherwise be accessible to women. Education expands opportunities for women, equips them to be more informed, empowers them to resist oppression and enables them to claim their rights. Women power, especially in rural areas, has been grossly underrated. The rural women may not be highly qualified but their wisdom cannot be doubted; they may not be physically very strong but their mental strength and readiness to work hard speak volumes about their character. Finally, they may not be professionally trained but their extra ordinary skills and interpersonal abilities cannot be doubted. Indian women have far greater visibility and voice than what they had 50 years ago. They have entered into and created impacts in every sphere of public activity. On the one hand, women must continue to claim rights and spaces for themselves, to enter new arenas of decision making, to participate in setting the agenda as well as discussing agendas set by others. Women's presence and participation are now recognised as an essential condition for development in some soft sectors like primary education, health, sanitation, etc. Men and women must work together to ensure rights and freedom for all citizens. But still there is a lot to do to uplift the women.

Education is not a way to escape poverty, it is a way of fighting it. Poverty is much more complex than simply income deprivation. It entails lack of empowerment, lack of knowledge and lack of opportunity as well as lack of income and capital. Despite increased access to education, the poor—disproportionately women, socially disadvantageous groups, the physically disabled, persons in remote regions—are often deprived of a basic education. And when basic education is available, the poorest are unable to avail to it because the direct and opportunity costs attached to it are quite high for them. For a majority of girls from poor rural families, going to school is an impossible dream. Only 54 percent of Indian women are literate as compared to 70 percent men. Grassroots women's groups should be empowered and encouraged to implement selected poverty alleviation schemes, particularly food-for-work schemes in areas affected by natural disasters.[4] A woman having financial freedom but not having formal / informal education cannot get empowerment in true spirit. The rights of a person whether man or woman or even child are protected, if the concerned person is alert, having knowledge of laws given to him in the Constitution and laws made by central and state governments. Paper work fight can succeed through formal and informal education and good discussion power. Even if you buy any product from the market, education helps you to get the knowledge about that product. Aiming at empowering the literate girls and women from the lower income households, there should be commitment to improve the lot of the underprivileged section of society, and impart information technology related vocational skills to young girls and women. Equal emphasis should also be given to personality development and language skills in these training programmes so that their employment potential is improved. Emphasis should be placed on overall personality development of the girls and women, including communication, assertion and negotiation skills. Good care should be taken to maintain the quality of education by the use of infrastructure and by requisitioning of service of qualified professionals. Study tours should be organised regularly to familiarise the students with the functioning and set-up of various services such as postoffice, police station and also to meet with well-known public figures, which will be educative for those who pursue it with this outlook.

In poor families, both boys and girls begin to help in household chores from a very early age, but as they grow older, the burden on girls increases disproportionately. By the time they reach adolescence, girls carry a major share of the burden of survival tasks including fetching water, collecting fuel, wood and fodder, cooking cleaning and caring for younger ones. Women represent a major force, a dormant volcano, a repository of immense potential and abilities. Empowerment of women through education, economic freedom and entrepreneurship can lead to the revolutionary era of development of human resource.

Moreover, parents must change their attitude towards their daughters and bring them up in a way that reflects equality. Daughters must be given opportunities to develop their decision-making skills and leadership capacities, and sons must be taught to respect their sister as equals. In particular, daughters must have equal access to the same quantity, quality and type of education as sons. The education system must be transformed to ensure that the content and process of education reflect gender equality.

Many girls and women need economic security due to various reasons. One of the main reason being their family responsibilities. In the context of the present state of society where the structure and shape of the family have undergone radical changes, economic needs have assumed great significance. However, charity begins at home. The educated women today can contribute a lot in uplifting the cause of other women. They can also contribute for the upliftment of their family and their standard of living by gaining access to employment opportunities that come their way. They can choose the profession of their career of choice. Educated girls are expected to contribute to the family income so as to meet the growing economic needs of the family. Moreover, educated girls can make use of their education for the economic betterment of their family.

Employment also contributes to the upgradation of status in the family as well as in the society. The relationship between education and poverty reduction is thus quite straight and linear as education is empowering, it enables the person to participate in the development process, it inculcates the knowledge and skills needed to improve the income earning potential and in turn the quality of life. Moreover education of girls and women helps in improving the number of other indicators of human development. The continuing challenge for women is to ensure that all women have the knowledge and skills necessary for continuing human and economic development and for breaking the poverty cycle.

Education will empower women as follow:

- It opens up avenues of communication that would otherwise be closed, expands personal choice and control over women's environment.
- It gives women access to information through both print and electronic media, equips them to cope better with work and family responsibilities.
- It strengthens their self-confidence to participate in community affairs and influence political issues.
- It gives disadvantaged women the tools they need to move from exclusion to full participation in society.
- It empowers the entire nation because educated women have the skills to make democratic institutions function effectively to meet the demands for a more sophisticated workforce, to work for a cleaner environment and to meet their social obligations as wives and mothers.

The Education Policy of 1986 emphasizes on education, training and improving the working skills of women. The average literacy rate in India has gone up from 52.21 percent in 1991 to 65.38 percent in 2001. The male literacy rate is 75.85 percent and female literacy rate is 54.16 percent. The government has taken several measures to improve women's education's levels in various areas like vocational education and skill development. The Tenth Five Year Plan (2002-07) focused on detailed vocational surveys, proper identification of marketable trade and strengthening vocational institutes with better linkage to industries. The Tenth Five Year Plan has also recognised the need for highly educated people including highly-killed scientists, engineers and managers in the Indian economy, and women are expected to play an important part in this development.[5] Investing in women's education results in substantial social and economic gains. Educated women have fewer children, have healthier children as well. Educating women has a stronger positive effect on children's health, education and welfare. Mothers are also more closely involved in the immediate care of children and in the critical decisions about food sanitation and general nutrition, all of which influence children's health and development. Women's education provides them great opportunities for employment and income, and raises the opportunity cost of these time in economic activities, compared to child rearing. An amount of Rs. 20,381,64 crore was spent on education by women related ministries / departments during the Ninth Five Year Plan period (1997-2002), and an amount of Rs. 1,497,35 crore was spent on science and technology for women during the same period. The other main ministries who spent 50.70 percent of their gross budget to support the Ninth Five Year Plan were family welfare, health and education. Labour and rural departments also contributed significantly.[6]

There has been increasing worldwide recognition and effort to improve and enhance the creativity, ability and contributions of women to the society; improve literacy among women; and reduced gender-based inequalities. There, have, however, been examples since ages, of outstanding performance and contributions of women in all most all fields, be it in science and technology, engineering, politics, literature, social sciences, music or industry. The enrolment of girls at the graduate level has gone up from 34.7 percent in 1990-91 to 40.9 percent in 1999-2000; at the postgraduate level from 32.8 percent it has gone up to 39.6

percent; at the Ph D/ D Sc / D Phil the percentage has gone up from 26.2 percent to 35.4 percent; engineering from 0.03 percent to 0.08 percent and MBBS from 0.03 percent to 0.05 percent of the total enrolments. For quite some time, we are hearing 30 percent reservation for women in different spheres like political / education / employment fronts. At the panchayati raj level, the government has already made amendments and the women have been given 30 percent reservation at the panchayat level. The bill for providing 30 percent reservation to women in parliament is pending for quite some time, and sincere efforts for passing the same and making constitutional amendments is required. In the education field since the year 2000, Maharashtra and many other states have implemented the rule of 30 percent reservation for women in colleges and professional institutions to provide education to them. Such a step is also required to be taken for the other remaining states for the upliftment of the women. Women are expected to share larger employment opportunities at higher management levels as these require less of physical inputs and more of intellectual capabilities. Women's education thus influences and is influenced by the context in which it is developed. Today, women's future is as bright as her past has been dark.

The Government of India has taken several measures to empower women including giving them educational facilities, employment and entrepreneurship opportunities. A National Knowledge Commission has been set up to enhance the knowledge-base and educational standards in the country. These examples have tended to establish the potential and capabilities of women which needed to be nurtured in the male-dominated society, not only to literate the women to be independent, but also to harness their abilities for the overall development. Education and economic independence are two great tools. Education can shape the life of a person. We have to give more and more education to our daughters. According to Jawaharlal Nehru, education teaches the person how to live in life. Link with education is economic power. Women should be economically independent so that may prove their worth.

When we look around we can see for ourselves that with each year passing, the number of womenfolk is increasing in the working class. Their literacy rate is also improving. The school results for the CBSE exams have proved in the past many years that girls are excelling better than the boys. There is high density competition between men and women vying for top positions in an organisation. All this has compelled the general populace to understand the importance of providing the proper status to their womenfolk. There is plentiful of literature available on various aspects of development and performances of women's education in modern societies; literature is also available for topics related to policies, governmental and non-governmental organisations' networks, support systems and other facilities available. This literature indicates the marked improvements in women's education levels and their positions in different fields over years but they still lag far behind men in many areas. All this and many more fields like computers, medicine, engineering and architecture have many from the fairer sex holding importance positions.

A survey reveals that women's overall share of management jobs rarely exceeds 20 percent. It is often seen that the greater the position, the more glaring is the gender gap. It is hard to believe that in the largest and powerful of organisations, the number of women acquiring the top position is usually less than 2 to 3 percent. According to the ILO, "Women represented more than 40 percent of the world's labour force in 1997-98, yet of their management positions remained unacceptably low." However, as we move to the knowledge-based societies with the rapid advances in technology, women are likely to increase their share in management areas, science and technology, industry, etc. It is evident that women empowerment has begun but at a minuscule level. The bottom line is that the basic thinking process has to change to enable a better status to the women of our land. It certainly is a long-drawn process as also an uphill task what with the traditional beliefs, tenets of the society and the basic mindset. But a step has been taken towards reformation which needs to be supported by each one of us. However the fact that women have certain characteristics, gifted by nature, particularly, physical and emotional, which are different from men in many ways, and the need for family or social balances, need to be kept in mind. Women, therefore, may have greater opportunities to perform managerial functions in the emerging knowledge economy, requiring more of intellectual inputs than physical work. A large number of women entrepreneurs of eminence have emerged in recent years, besides women occupying senior management positions in large companies and MNCs.

The Constitution of India is the Magna Carta for the women of India. For them, the centuries of slavery are over. Indian womanhood is on the march. They are coming into their own. Today women enjoy equal status with men. After 55 years of independence, position of Indian women is much more bright and prosperous. Indian women have far better visibility and voice than visible in the pre-independence era. Their presence can be felt in every sphere of life, be it in professional field like medicine and engineering, be it politics or be it in other social areas. Women are more and more involved in decision making. It has been accepted that women in India are a tremendous workforce which is utilised far below its potential.

Globalisation and the increasing impact of technology mean more opportunities for women than ever before. However, this can also cause increasing problems for those not prepared to think differently and creativity in an increasingly competitive world. Planning and strategy insist that without education it is not possible to have a perfect view of the future, and education will generate a perfect level of future knowledge. Today creativity is seen throughout the world as an driving force for competitive advantage, and the main creative competencies are related to innovation, judgment, opportunity recognition, relationship building and proactive, which, acting together, will give women a distinct competitive edge. Whether you are a working woman or a housewife, it is important for you keep abreast of trends and changes in the world today and that gives you the competitive edge in a dynamic world.

A large percentage of women in our country have a low literacy level, and are shy of dealing with outsiders, and thus have economic dependence on male counterpart. They have the potential to be successful in every walk of life. They have the aspiration to excel and capacity to work hard. Those who meet the challenge and build character within themselves are surely the ones who will be able to respond with swiftness and effectiveness. They who optimise their work are the ones who will be able to move beyond a state of survival to a growth.

Contradictions exist in every society, and ours is also no exception. The woman in the hut has no idea that her lot is supposed to improve with each passing year. She has no idea that women are supposedly on the move in her own country. And that they're hurtling ahead at such breathtaking speed, men are unable to keep pace. When she does leave the prescribed space to work in the fields, she makes sure her face is covered from the eyes of the prying world. More importantly, a woman should know how to handle herself and not lose heart. She must remember that she's still in contention for a place in the national squad. It's also a question of her reputation, so she must be well prepared.

Women's Education is an Investment that will Never Fail

It is a well proved fact that economic development, social development and education are interdependent, and we can't achieve sustainable development and will fail in our efforts to achieve a higher quality of life for the population at large when any one of these is missing. It is the endeavour of the government and the political leaders to remove all the obstacles to women's active participation in all spheres of life through a full and equal share in economic, social, cultural and political decision-making, which is possible only when the womenfolk are educated. Every real life situation brings up new twists and turns and creates new problems. Education will help us in building an ability to master these twists and turns and help us to break free of hesitations. It helps us to achieve the ability to say something appropriate in the everyday situations we face in our social and career life. Education will help us look at ourselves, moving closer to the truth of who we are. In doing so, we move beyond the limitations of our personality, and the world around us begins to transform. Once that happens, we are on our way to achieving higher and higher levels. The space it occupies in our lives is not new or recently created. It promises the younger generation at life's crossroads the healing and transforming touch and also brings a new confidence in them. There's no alternative to our interest in achieving true education, which will help us to do what we want to achieve. If so, there are certain things we will have to do on our own sooner or later.

School education is the first and most promising milestone towards self-realisation and reflects where we are in our journey towards the ultimate. It is quite different to what it was yesterday, and has done a tremendous effort—to remove the stigma. We need to make it a vehicle for social and economic emancipation today. Moral education is all important. From their earliest years children must be taught the difference between right and wrong, and trained to love and follow what is right, and hate and avoid what is wrong. Such training means the formation of character on the right lines. Its object is to bring children up in such a way that they will grow up to be truth-loving, honest, brave, pure-minded and unselfish men and women. The purpose of education should be to give an exposure of different aspects of art and cultural heritage, people and religion. This will help in developing the character, courage and cooperative spirit in the women of nation. We desperately need more schools affecting a very large number of women and girls.

We have all gone through life saying certain things about ourselves. We are not the same persons we were yesterday—since then we have had numerous interactions, learned things we did not know, and had experiences we had not before. We are conscious of what we know. Memories, experiences, knowledge, information from the past remain in our subconscious. Everyone is aware that there is something beyond one's knowledge but has never experienced it. There are no failures in life. There are only learning experiences. Education enhances the brain's powers of concentration and its ability to quickly change its train of thoughts. Learning is an investment for a healthy future. It is fast becoming a mass movement, and we need policies that enable the revolution to spread much faster in women creating new propositions. Exhibiting a balanced combination of education with an eagerness to change and innovate will be a window of opportunity.

The goals of women's education should mainly be to minimise symptoms such as depression, agitation and suspiciousness and providing psychological interventions, counsel women on birth preparedness, safe delivery, breast-feeding, immunisation, contraception and prevention of common infections. Education helps us in galvanising the subconscious to forge intuitive, creative and broader perception for resolving the problem and coming out of the ignorance about ourselves. The goal is always visible but yet we approach it and retreat from it several times, often turning away to reconsider our stance; education will help us find our way to the goal. It will provide an opportunity to employ a perspective both creative and effective to leverage and focus the strength of imagination for drawing ourselves into positive solution and sources, to decipher the constraints and recurrences of our life for gaining access to greater energy and consciousness.

Education had to be a continuous process and the skills had to be constantly upgraded. The education guides people by developing necessary skills, knowledge and outlook. The success of a focused strategy is evident. It creates an environment where all can fulfil their dreams along with meeting objectives. It enables performance empowered with authority and responsibility, and ensures the performance is fair, transparent, balanced and motivating because values and believes revolve around excellence, honesty, knowledge, caring, integrity and teamwork. "Knowledge of the Self is the one direct means for emancipation. As fire is necessary for cooking, so without knowledge of the Self there can be no emancipation. Action or *karma* cannot destroy ignorance – knowledge does. The Supreme Soul appears finite on account of ignorance. But when that ignorance is destroyed, verily that one Atma or Soul shines by itself like the sun when the clouds are dispelled" (*Adi Sankara, Atma Bodha* 2-4). Education is an important institution in any modern or modernising society. Historically education has passed practically every sphere of human life. Learning in India, through the ages, was sought not for its own sake, but for the sake and as a part of religion. It was regarded as a means of salvation or self-realisation, as the means to the highest end of life, viz., *mukti* or emancipation. It is therefore obvious that ancient Indian education is to be understood as being ultimately the product of Indian theory of knowledge and corresponding scheme of life and values.

Education is after all a means of making wishes come true. Its primary work is to release body, mind, heart and spirit towards great purposes. It communicate to people their worth and potential so clearly that they are inspired to see it in themselves. It facilitates the way for helping people to optimise their capacities and potential. It allows people to fulfil their purpose and contribution for the benefit of both individual and society. These principles are the foundation for creating lives. It creates certain responsibilities to be discharged to the best of our abilities. It will help us in planning to obtain the best synergies to meet the challenges of the present phase of globalisation and at the same time, take advantage of all the opportunities that are available. It helps in taking meaningful steps to establish coordination between procedures and timeframe implementation of measures; they would take care of all the woes. There is a dearth of good vocational courses and training and the government should take steps towards restructuring training and carrying out capacity-building programmes to face the emerging challenges.

Only when we are willing to accept that our words are creative, our thoughts are creative, and our actions are creative, these will produce our highest visions. Education initiates us to speak, think, and act in a way of which we can be proud of, and will move us through the most difficult moments in our life into peace and equanimity and even serenity. This is the most important part of our life and our activities because it is the process by which we create our lives. Education will help women to make their own day, and do so with confidence and courage. There is no celebration in the lives of those women who have no access to education, to personal liberties, even to their own thoughts. Their lives remain exactly where their grandmothers lives once were. Women are no novice and they know what their shortcomings are. All they need is the determination to do well. If they cannot see the writing on the wall, no one else can do it for them. Every question they ever have in their lives will be answered. What they need is to first acquaint themselves with the various issues in detail. Education will amplify the energy manifold and could have a different impact in different areas. It will provide with an indepth understanding of society, will update us on a range of knowledge and skills of our interest. It will help women to contribute better to the nation and society and will be more determined than ever to make it big by spelling out their priorities with much more vigour and doing follow-ups till some action is taken. A holistic approach has to be adopted. Capabilities will get a significant boost, with the new thinking. They are not going to keep quite and to say that time will solve the problem. The government must create opportunities for economic development and building a society based on the ideals of our national leaders who visualised a nation based on a just social order. Their thought process and methodology of action must be adopted for bringing about a societal transformation.

There is great scope of consolidate growth momentum with special emphasis on education and employment generation for women. It is our endeavour to revive and improve the feeling of "involvement". There is an urgent need to give the whole issue a rethink and decide on what the future should behold. The education of "quality and truth" could widen the scope of knowledge and inspire pupils to inculcate positive values. The teachers should treat this as one of their important social responsibilities. Education is a thought, a principle, a way of life, a movement. Our aim should be to clear the cobwebs in women's mind and bring about a change in the mindset and the common perception. It is a thoughtful guide on how the governance can be improved, and how women themselves can play an important role in taking control of the rules that control their lives. Nothing could compensate for it.

There are just so many opportunities to make education more functional. Our education system needs serious rebuilding. Ours is a system that is more or less based on grades and degrees, emphasizing the role of education and legislation to solve the problems of society. Education creates a level playing field. But all this can happen only if there is a policy roadmap backed by legislation. There is a general climate of transformation for better. It's the same mission as searching for life on Mars. The major challenge to the humanities today is in exploring the radically novel and critical ways of relating or associating the human articulations. Knowledge is not mandatory; all we need is a mature viewpoint. All of us have a mature viewpoint and a sustained level of intelligence. A person with a balanced state of mind always seems to cement the relationship. That's all necessary to be truly awakened; that we can consciously participate in the life process. Our thoughts have a direct influence on the way we feel and behave, and we are all needed by our very own self. We can use visualisation to harness the energy of our imagination. Education lays the foundation for better decision-making and communication. We need to have more confidence in ourselves and our ability to beat the best in the world. "Education should help people to build up self-confidence and self-reliance based on balanced human relationship."[1] Education will help women in believing every human being is born to fulfil certain duties. They should never lose faith themselves, and perhaps this will give them the strength to perform well and prove themselves. Once women get that confidence, the 'white' fixation will automatically vanish and will really be able to forge ahead.

The government should vigorously pursue educational reforms which may be helpful in yielding positive results. The delivery of social services including education and health, which would help in the irradiation of the stigma of illiteracy in the womenfolk and to become part and parcel of the process of economic development of the nation. In society people have a duty also to help one another. Women have an important role to play in this transformation process. The success or failure of the human race has always depended more on women than on men. The future will be determined by inspiration in everything we do. None can offer more inspiration to others than he actually feels in himself as human beings have the free will to override their own natural instincts.

Depending on how you act in every lifetime, you are either accumulating positive or negative attitude. Today's woman definitely knows what she wants. She's no longer cowed down by the thought that she's staying in a male-dominated environment, which perhaps, in certain ways, she still is. Much of the change has come about due to education and the emerging economic independence for the women. In the past, a woman's sacred duty was to get married and have children. Her identity was limited, as even at home, she often didn't have a voice. Eventually, a feeling of worthlessness crept into her psyche. As she steps outside the safety of her house and make a mark in her, she has a chance to prove her worth. She must just try to stand up and show that she isn't scared or has no fear. But words don't count for anything. It's the actions that really matters. What we learned from the experience is that the more we put ourselves in a winning position, the more we are likely to win. If we do not meet the challenge to continue to give a competitive service others will emerge that will replace ours. As we face challenges and move through difficulties, many times we feel lonely, isolated or misunderstood by others. Our old patterns of thinking and doing don't give us the guidance we need to actualise our ideals and transform our lives. It would be unforgivable to refuse to improve the capacity. We need a means of funding our way through the day-to-day reality of living in the way that supports our desires.

Education will get rid women of the problem of the day and will bring them fully into the present.

Nothing succeeds like success, true but how many of us really succeed in that mission? A joyful and pleasant life is all about the healthy and winning outcomes, the major challenge for all of us is to know our real potential, create enough passion in our lives, and ignite the dormant energies, capacities and intellect to put ourselves onto a dream path. With a well structured path to bring fulfilment and meaningfulness to their lives, education also helps them to remove mental fog and haze to realise their dreams, and act with confidence and conviction. Mahatma Gandhi was very sensitive towards the problems of women. He considered the women among the weakest and most deprived in society. Education can't deliver results overnight but it is only a part of the larger learning process. Nothing can change in a day or two. It cannot change you overnight but it gives something new to think about, some new experiences. Recovery embodies the process of reclaiming hope, humanity, equality and dignity—birthrights that women were stripped by society at large. They were denied the opportunity to express their views, and to introspect and analyse their performance. There is a need to stem the tide through a tremendous amount of awareness building through education, and this should be our immediate objective. If we don't realise this, we fail to harness women power.

References

1. Planning Commission, Government of India, *Draft Fifth Five Year Plan*, 1974-79, New Delhi, p. 193.
2. Uttam Kumar Singh, *Women Educations*, Commonwealth Publishers, New Delhi, 1997, p. 3.
3. Jasprit Kaur Soni, *Women Empowerment: Exploring the Fact*, Authorspress, New Delhi, 2006, p.115.
4. *Approach Paper to the Tenth Five Year Plan (2002-2007)*, Planning Commission, Government of India, New Delhi, September, 2001, p.30.
5. *The Tenth Five Year Plan 2002-07; Women and Children*; Planning Commission, New Delhi.
6. Ibid.

4

Profile of the Universe

RAJASTHAN

Rajasthan is socially and economically backward state. It ranks around 13 among 17 major states regarding most of the indicator of socio-economic development. The state is suffering from several natural handicaps as almost 60 per cent of its area lies in the Thar Desert. The economy of Rajasthan predominantly depends upon agriculture. However, the industrial structure of Rajasthan is changing steadily.

At present Rajasthan is a political and administrative entity. In the process of its development the state has retained several ethnicities which it had enjoyed as an autonomous princely state. Before the present integration of the princely state of Rajasthan there were 21 princely states. Each state was autonomous. The history of Rajasthan dates back to the pre-historic times. Around 3,000 and 1,000 BC, it had a culture akin to that of the Indus Valley Civilisation. It was the Chauhans who dominated Rajput affairs from seventh century and by twelfth century they had become an imperial power. After the Chauhans, it was the Guhilots of Mewar who controlled the destiny of the warring tribes. Besides Mewar, the other historically prominent states were Marwar, Jaipur, Bundi, Kota, Bharatpur and Alwar. Other states were only offshoots of these. All these states accepted the British Treaty of Subordinate Alliance in 1818 protecting the interest of the princes. This naturally left the people discontented.

It has its own language, customs, history and rules of marriage. The cultural regions of Rajasthan are coterminous with the linguistic region. Some of the cultural regions of the region include Dundhar where the people speak dhundhari language.

Then there is a Mewat cultural region where the dialect spoken is Mewati. Perhaps the largest cultural region in the state is the Marwar where Marwari is the language of the people. The region of Mewar is held together by the Mewari language. The southern region of Rajasthan is known as Vagad or Vagar where the people speak a language that is the mixture of Gujarati and Mewari. Rajasthan, the largest state in India (3, 287,263 Sq. Km.) with an area of 3, 42, 239 sq. kms., constituting about 10.4 per cent of the total geographical area of the country prior to independence, was known as Rajputana or the home of Rajputs – a martial community who ruled over this area for centuries.

After the revolt of 1857, the people united themselves under the leadership of Mahatma Gandhi to contribute to the freedom movement. With the introduction of provincial autonomy in 1935 in British India, agitation for civil liberties and political rights became stronger in Rajasthan. The process of uniting scattered states commenced from 1948 to 1956 when the States Reorganisation Act was promulgated. First came Matsya Union (1948) consisting of a fraction of states. Slowly and gradually other states merged with this Union. By 1949, major states like Bikaner, Jaipur, Jodhpur and Jaisalmer joined this Union making it United States of Greater Rajasthan. Ultimately in 1958, the present state of Rajasthan formally came into being, with Ajmer state, the Abu Road Taluka and Sunel Tappa joining it. The entire western flank of the state borders with Pakistan, while Punjab, Haryana, Uttar Pradesh and Madhya Pradesh bind Rajasthan in north, north-east and south-east and Gujarat in south-west.

As per the Census of 1991, the total population of Rajasthan is 440, 06 lakhs of whose S. T. population is 54.75 lakhs constituting 12.44 per cent of the total population. Sex wise females constitute 50 per cent of total population. As per Census 2001, the total population of Rajasthan is 56,473,122 including women population 27,091,465.[1] But development among women shows a dismaying picture. No nation can march forward by ignoring half of its population. Women can play a leading and participatory role in the development and national building programmes. This can only be achieved when the status of women is brought on par with that of men. For a long time Indian society has been treating the women-folk as the lowest among the lowest in social status. But nowadays they have come forward to get their share of social status. So is the case of tribal women who have many privileges as compared to other women like enjoying freedom in all sphere of life. But they were debarred from making important decisions, participating in several religious rituals. They cannot act as religious or political heads.

Agriculture

The total cultivable area in the state is 159 lakh hectares (2001-02). The estimated food grain production is 124,49 lakh tone. The principal crops cultivated in the state are rice, barley, jowar, millet, maize, gram, wheat, oilseeds, pulses, cotton and tobacco. Cultivation of vegetable and citrus fruits such as orange and malta has also picked up over the last few years. Other crops are red chillies, mustard, cuminseed, fenugreek and asafoetidal.

Industry and Minerals

Endowed with a rich culture, Rajasthan is also rich in minerals and is fast emerging on the industrial scenario of the country. Some of the important central undertakings are Zinc Smelter Plant at Debari (Udaipur), Copper Plant at Khetri Nagar (Jhunjhunu) and Precision Instrument Factory at Kota. Small-scale industrial units numbering 22,97 lakh with a capital investment of Rs 3,296 crore provided employment potential to about 8,86 lakh persons in the State as on January 2002. Major industries are textiles and woollens, sugar, cement, glass, sodium plants, oxygen, vegetable dyes, pesticides, zinc, fertilisers, railway wagons, ball bearings, water and electricity metres, sulphuric acid, television sets, synthetic yarn and insulating bricks. Besides, precious and semi-precious stones, caustic soda, calcium carbide, nylon and tyres, etc., are other important industrial units.

Rajasthan has rich deposits of zinc concentrates, emerald, garnet, gypsum, silver ore, asbestos, feldspar and mica. The state also abounds in salt, rock phosphate, marble and red stone deposits. The first Efport Promotion Industrial Park of the country has been established and made operational at Sitapura (Jaipur).

Irrigation and Power

The irrigation potential has been raised by 19,185 hectares during 2001-02 and the total irrigation potential of the state is 28, 85 lakh hectares. The state purchased 1,234,188 crore units of power in addition to its own generation of 1,286.0,68 crore units of power during 2001-02.

Transport

The total length of roads was 88,801 km as on March 2002.

Railways

Jodhpur, Jaipur, Bikaner, Kota, Sawai Madhopur and Bharatpur are main rail junctions of the state.

Aviation

Regular air services connect Jaipur, Jodhpur and Udaipur with Delhi and Mumbai.

High Court

Jodhpur.

Tourist Centres

Jaipur, Jodhpur, Udaipur. Bikaner, Mount Abu, Sariska, Tiger Century in Alwar, Keoladeo National Parkat Bharatpur, Ajmer, Jaisalmer, Pali and Chittorgarh are important places of tourist interest in the state.

Districts

1. Ajmer 2. Alwar 3. Banswara 4. Barmer 5. Bharatpur 6. Bhilwara 7. Bikaner 8. Bundi 9. Chittorgarh 10. Churu 11. Dholpur 12. Dungarpur 13. Ganganagar 14. Jaipur 15. Jaisalmer 16. Jalore 17. Jhalwar 18. Jhunjhunu 19. Jodhpur 20. Kota 21. Nagaur 22. Pali 23. Sawai Madhopur 24. Sikar 25. Sirohi 26. Tonk 27. Udaipur 28. Dausa 29. Baran 30. Rajsamund 31. Hanumangarh 32. Karoli.[2]

Rajasthan has the distinction of being the leader in atrocities and violation of human rights. As per Census 2001 it has also the distinction of being in the first position in achieving the highest decadel difference of literacy rate of India. Udaipur District has achieved the first position in Rajasthan urban literacy rate of 86.19 and Udaipur city has topped with a literacy rate of 87.90 per cent including male literacy of 94.10 per cent and female literacy rate of 81.02 per cent. Three out of five tehsils having highest urban literacy in Rajasthan are in Udaipur district. Two out of five tehsils with the lowest literacy are also from the district of Udaipur with Kotra registering 24.52 per cent literacy rate being the lowest with 37.51 per cent male literacy and 11.14 per cent female literacy. So it can be observed from the data that Udaipur district has a varied picture in its literacy position.

Udaipur

Maharana Udai Singh II founded Udaipur in 1568 after his citadel Chittorgarh was sacked by Mughal Emperor Akbar. Legends say that Udai Singh was guided by a holy man meditating on the hill near Pichola Lake to establish his capital on this very spot. Surrounded by Aravali Ranges, forests and lakes this place was less vulnerable than Chittorgarh. Maharana Udai Singh died in 1572 and was succeeded by Maharana Pratap who valiantly defended Udaipur from subsequent Mughal attacks. Maharana Pratap is the most revered Rajput icon who gallantly fought the Mughals at the Haldighati in 1576. Mewar continuously defied foreign invaders and has a history of bloody battles until the British intervention in the nineteenth when a treaty was signed to protect Udaipur. Upon independence Udaipur merged with the Union of India. The district is named after the principal city Udaipur which was founded by Rana Udai Singh in about 1959 AD.

Udaipur district is located in south central Rajasthan. It is located between latitudes 23'46 to 25'05 North and longitudes 73'09 to 74'35 East. It shares its boundaries with six other districts of Rajasthan. It is bounded on the north by Rajsamand district, on the south by Dungarpur and Banswara district, on the east by Chittourgarh district and on the west by Pali and Sirohi district.

Udaipur district is located in southern part of Rajasthan and covers an area of 12,498 square kilometres which is 3.64 per cent of the total area of state of Rajasthan. The population of Udaipur district is 19.98 lakh. Here about 85 per cent of total population lives in villages and about 54 per cent belongs to Scheduled Castes / Scheduled Tribes. The total working force of the district is nearly 33 per cent of the total population. The district is very rich in live stock resources as well as mineral resources, yet it is industrially backward. In Udaipur district, two employment exchanges are entrusted with the work of registration and placement of unemployment persons.

a) The first Employment Exchange is situated in Amba Mata. The registrants with it includes a wide range of unemployed-illiterate, up to middle, matric, higher secondary, senior higher secondary, graduate and the post-graduate in third division.

b) The second Employment Exchange is situated in Science College, Udaipur. The registrants with it are post-graduates in I or II division and other technically qualified persons like doctors, engineers, scholars, etc.

Our universe of study is Udaipur district in the state of Rajasthan having the population 26,32,210 of which 21,42,068 (81.38 per cent) lives in rural area and 4,90,142 (18.62 per cent) lives in urban area (according to Census 2001). Udaipur district ranks 17th in the position of urban population being 23.38 per cent, having a literacy rate 59.26 per cent with rural literacy rate 52.52 per cent and urban 86.19 per cent. Development of masses of rural areas depends upon the motivation, awareness, health and knowledge about the programmes formulated by the government for the upliftment of rural masses.

Total workers	:	1,101,715 (female-412,771, 31.82 %)
Main workers	:	724,178 (female- 151,363, 11.67 %)
Marginal workers	:	377,537 (female-261,408, 20.15%)
Total Non Worker	:	1,530,495 (female-884,422, 68.18%)[3]

According to Census 2001 out of the total population of Udaipur there are 1,101,715 total workers having 112,771 female workers out of which 724,178 are main workers, having 151,363 female as main workers and 377,537, marginal workers having 261,408 female marginal workers. Out of total population the number of non-workers is 1,530,495 out of which 884,422 are female. Out of total female population 68.18 per cent are non-workers and 31.82 per cent are in workers category out of which 11.67 per cent, 20.15 per cent are main workers and marginal workers respectively.[4] The 1991 Census recorded a total population of 2086,255 with 1,690,422 living in rural and 365,079 living in urban areas. According to Census 2001 Udaipur has total population 2,632,210 out of which 2,142,068 live in rural areas and has 490,142 urban population.[5] Udaipur district has the second highest population figure in Rajasthan. Udaipur has a high concentration of tribal population. Tribal, mainly Bhil Adivasi, account for 46.19 per cent of the total population of the district.

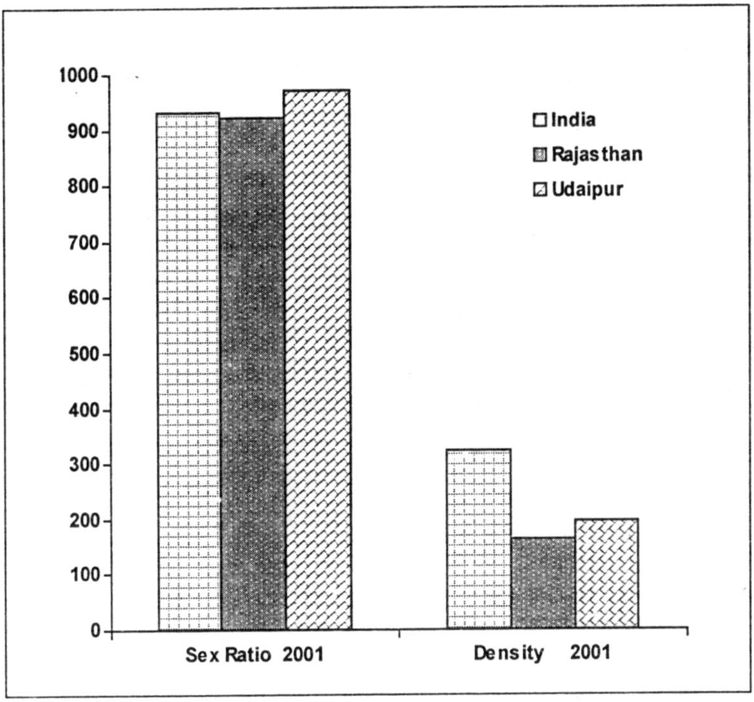

Graph 4.1 : A Comparative Scenario - I
(Sex Ratio & Density)

Udaipur is also known as the 'City of Lakes'. The city hailed as the 'Venice of the East' is set amidst the Aravali hills of Southern Rajasthan. It is one of the most romantic destinations in India. Udaipur has a profusion of marble palaces, lakes, temples, cenotaphs and rugged hills. It is also proud of its heritage as a centre for the performing arts, painting and crafts. Udaipur is a major tourist place in Rajasthan. Together with the marble industry, tourism is the biggest industry of the city.

Udaipur district was last delimited on the 11 April 1991. It is now composed of 10 tehsils. Earlier it had 17 tehsils, but seven now belong to the newly created district Rajsamand. Udaipur district comprises 11 blocks. Most of them are identical with the tehsils.

From the above graph we find that the sex ratio of Udaipur is 972 is much higher to the national sex ratio 933 with Rajasthan having a sex ratio of 922.[6] The density of Udaipur according to the 2001 Census is 196 persons per sq km. as compared to 165 persons per sq km. of Rajasthan.[7]

Facts and Figures

Population	:	26, 32,210
Sex ratio	:	972:1000
Total workers	:	1,101,715
Main workers	:	724,178
Marginal workers	:	377,537
Village	:	2225
Literacy	:	59.26
Rainfall	:	61cm
Roads	:	280 K.M.
Tehsils	:	10
Best season	:	Throughout the year
STD code	:	0294

Temperature

Summer: Max: 33.3°C Min: 23.3°C

Winter: Max: 28.3°C Min: 11.6°C

Table 4.1

Statistical Chart Udaipur (1991 Census)

Area	12,596.00
Population	20, 86,255.00
Rural	16,90, 422.00
Urban	3,65,079.00
Census town	30, 684.00
Scheduled Castes	6.61

(Contd...)

(Contd...)

Scheduled Tribes	46.19
Female ratio (per thousand males)	972.00
Density of population	179.00
Urban area	5.00
Villages	2,248.00
Electrified villages	2,035.00
Lok Sabha constituencies	2.00
Vidhan Sabha constituencies	10.00
Tesils	10.00
Sub-tehsils	6.00
L.R. circle	43.00
Patwar mandals	389.00
Panchayat samiti	11.00
Gram panchayats	498.00
Area under cultivation('000hec)	357.03
Land holding (Avg.)	1.68
Percentage of area sown to total area 14.40	
Average rainfall (C. M.)	65.25
Wells	11,725.00
Animal husbandry hospitals	42.00
Dispensaries	17.00
Other centres	93.00
Cattle	2,536,504.00
Poultry	350,694.00

District Rural Development Agency, 22.8, 1995

Table 4.2

Unemployed Scenario

(In Lakh)

Particulars	*India*	*Rajasthan*	*Udaipur*
No. of Persons	8441.0	440.0	19.98
Unemployed	363.0	9.02	0.52
Persons	(4.3 %)	(2.0 %)	(3.6 %)

Census of India 1991

— Police Administration:	
Dy. S. P. Circle	7
Police Stations	37
Police Outposts	43
— Road Classification (Kms.) :	3,037
— National Highway No. 8	108
— State Highway	433
— District Roads :	1,131
— Rural Roads :	1,365
— Metalled Roads : (per 1000 sq.km)	204.98

Table 4.3

Roads Scenario

Road (Kms.)	3,037
National highway	108
State highway	433
District roads	1,131
Rural roads	1,365
Metalled roads (per 1000 sq.km)	204.98

Decadal growth rate of population o Udaipur is 27.37 as compare to Rajasthan 28.33.[8]

Literacy	*34.80*
Male:	24.70
Female:	20.30
Rural:	24.70
Urban:	76.01

Table 4.4

Educational Institutions

Primary Schools	1744
Upper Primary (Middle) Schools	396
Secondary / Hr. Secondary Schools	195
Colleges (General)	8

Table 4.5
Health Centres

Medical & Health Hospitals (Allopathy)	16
Dispensaries	10
P.H.C.	79
Sub-centres	475
T. B. Clinic	1
Ayurvedic	175
Homoepathic	6
Unani	2

— Sub-divisions: 4
(Jhadol, Vallabhnagar, Salumbar, Girwa)

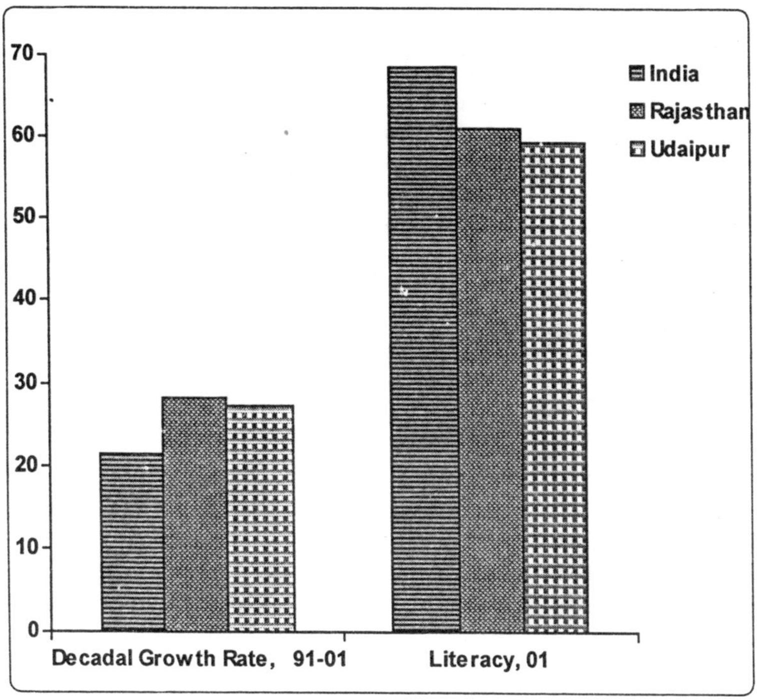

Graph 4.2
A Comparative Scenario – II
(Decadal Growth & Literacy)

Government Development Activities

The government rural development activities consists of development schemes (IRDP, Indira Awas Yojana, etc.) designed and financed at central or state government level. These schemes are administered by the DRDA under the chairmanship of the District Collector. In Udaipur district, as in other districts in Rajasthan, the panchayats are involved in the identification of beneficiaries for the various DRDA schemes. However, their involvement is often limited and their decisions may be superseded by administrative authorities.

Besides the DRDA schemes, various state government departments (Department of Agriculture, Department of Education etc.) are represented with a branch in Udaipur district and are also involved in rural development.

In Udaipur district, the Tribal Area Development Department under the authority of the Division Commissioner co-ordinates and monitors development activities related to tribal welfare and development. The programmes are implemented by government agencies and increasingly Non-Governmental Organisations (NGOs). The Tribal Area Development Department also recommends new programmes for tribal development but does not implement works. Udaipur has one of 14 Tribal Research Institutes in India. The institute is under the authority of the Tribal Welfare Department.

References

1. Census of India, Rajasthan, *Series-9, Paper-3,* 2001. p. xi.
2. Census of India, Rajasthan, *Series-9, Paper-2,* 2001, pp.7-20.
3. *Series-9, Paper-3,* op. cit., pp.74-158.
4. Ibid.
5. Ibid., p. 158.
6. *Series-9, Paper-2,* 2001. op. cit., pp. 81-82.
7. Census of India, Rajasthan, *Series-9, Paper-1,* 2001. p.45.
8. Ibid, p.39.

5

Profile of the Sample Population

Women's education can be defined as a revolution by which we can change and turn the older consensus. Mere regulations sometimes prevent women from getting education and get excluded or marginalised. Elements such as emotions and family values are included in their behaviour and this is like an air-filled balloon, which when pressurised can burst and it can be really good or really bad. We need to be sure that women's education is responsive to women's behaviour, and can serve us for empowerment and movement and for advancing women's human rights. In recent years the growing consensus and realisation of women's education has led to a heightened sense that women are always a party to every act of humanity. In the wake of this realisation, it has come to everyone's mind that real education is to be found in an effort to hear and attend to all the different voices of women. The present study is based on the interviews conducted with a sample of 100 females of Udaipur. One of the important and foremost components of research is to enable the reader to understand its effectiveness. The system should be evolved through a continuous updated process and only then, can the churn be properly measured and analysed.

A profile of the sample population is given below:

Age

Age may be an important factor contributing to status and prestige. The present study found that 28 per cent were in the younger age group, below 30 years. Age is a factor which plays an important role in participatory process. The age of an individual may be responsible to some extent to make the individual take an interest in the activities. The age composition of a population decides the structure of labour force. The rate of work participation differs in different age groups.[1]

Education

Every social thinker, economic scientist is of the opinion that the population crisis, poverty and shabby income conditions are mainly due to illiteracy of the masses. People nowadays are conscious about the education of their children. This is mainly due to the thrust and facilities given by the government. "Women can not only further their own cause and that of all minorities, but also help to shape the educational system of the 21st century." (Amy Lezberg). Education is considered to be an important mechanism for development in India, specially for women. Since women were traditionally and historically deprived of their basic right, education was far less away from their reach. Education is to promote the economic development of women and to protect them from social injustice and exploitation. Incentives have been provided by constitution to these sections, mainly in the sectors i.e. education, employment and reservation. The women have started to read and write. The speed is no doubt very slow, but women now realise the importance of education. The government provides all facilities to them for free education. Under the human rights educational interest of women is a special responsibility of central and State governments. The governments are, therefore, extending facilities in various shapes for the promotion of women's education.

Education faces the challenge of making the women understand its importance and effectiveness. There are, in truth, a great many things to say about this transformation. In the author's experience education without causing any defection from the social beliefs and culture will instil love in women, teach and value the changes associated with the present situation that will bring a real renovation, a widening of the field of knowledge and a deepened understanding of everything it contains. We must value the enrichment it supplies. Proponents of value education think it will protect women against lurking ill and gender-biased treatment, and presume that its contributions will help women in penetrating, monopoly of men on everything important to know.

Table 5.1: Educational Qualification with Age

	Under Matric	*%*	*Matric & Senior*	*%*	*Graduate*	*%*	*PG & Technical*	*%*	*Total*
20 to 30	1.00	3.57	3	10.71	9.00	32.14	15.00	53.58	28
%	14.29		25		27.27		31.25		
31 to 40	-	0	6	12.50	21.00	43.75	21.00	43.75	48
%			50		63.64		43.75		
41 to 50	6.00	25	3	12.50	3.00	12.5	12.00	50.00	24
%	85.71		25		9.09		25.00		
Total	7.00		12		33.00		48.00		100

After the age of 16 when education is no longer compulsory, young people have a variety of choice. Higher education is helpful in developing imagination and innovative solutions. Those who decide to stay on in education at the age of 16 usually move into higher education. Converting information into knowledge and wisdom is education. The author thinks education has been an issue that has been portrayed traditionally in this patriarchal society as a male arena. So sometimes women fear because they feel they cannot handle it, or they don't have the capacity to do it; that doesn't mean that most women are like that, because we have changed a lot of the culture and more and more women are empowered and are really using education to mobilise themselves. Out of 28 women in a age group of 20 to 30 only one(3.57%) was under matric, 3(10.71%) possessed senior certificates, nine(32.14%) were graduates and 15(53.58%) had post—graduate and technical degreesIn the age group of 31 to 40, out of 48 respondents none was under matric, 6(12.5%) had passed matric or senior secondary, 21((43.75%) of them had graduate degrees and same number of respondents possessed postgraduate or technical degrees. In the age group of 41 to 50, we clearly see that six(25%) out of 24 were under matric, 3(12.5%) were in possession of matric or senior certificates, same number of respondents were graduates and 12(50%) of them were postgraduates or had technical degrees. Out of seven under matriculates 1 was in the age group of 20 to 30 and 6(85.71%) were in age group of 41 to 50. Out of 12 respondents having matric or senior certificates 3 were in the age group of 20 to 30, 6 were in the age group 31 to 40 and 3 were in the age group of 41 to 50. Out of 33 graduates nine of were in the age group of 20 to 30, 21 were in age group 31 to 40 and only 3 were in the age group 41 to 50. Out of 48 respondents having post graduate or other technical degrees15, 21 and 15 were in the age group of 20 to 30, 31 to 40 and 41 to 50 respectively.

Table 5.2: Educational Qualification with Occupation

	Under Matric	*%*	*Matric & Senior*	*%*	*Graduate*	*%*	*PG & Technical*	*%*	
Studying					6	66.67	3	33.33	9
%					18.18		6.25		
House-hold	7	28	12	48	3	12	3	12	25
%	100		100		9.09		6.25		
Working					24	36.36	42	63.64	66
%					72.73		87.5		
Total	7		12		33		48		100

The decision of women about their work participation depends upon several social, cultural and economic factors. Education and their socio-cultural condition in society are the main factors determining the pattern of work participation. The women of today do not flee from challenges, but serve with honour even in adverse circumstances and successfully take everyone along; this testifies the inherent strength in them. Occupation is one of the important characteristics of status and prestige of a person. Besides a source of income, the occupation of a person is as good a clue to various aspects of his personality. A person's financial status in society and style of life, and class position depend upon his occupation.

Out of 100 respondents nine girls are pursuing further studies out of which six are in undergraduate courses and three are in post-graduate courses. Out of 100 respondents 25 respondents are householders; out of them seven are undermatric, 12 are matric and senior secondary, three are graduate and three are postgraduate or possess a technical degree. Diploma professional or technical education fields were male-dominated and represented women's lower education level, their less interest in professional or technical courses, skills, higher illiteracy rate and also sex segregation in education. Female literacy is still low in developing countries like India. Moreover, generally they do not go in the for or are not allowed to go in for higher education. Thus, the education level of women is low compared to men. If women opt for higher education then they often choose some sex typical courses, for example, courses in arts, fine arts, home science, medicine, etc. Girls usually do not choose technical education and if they go in for technical education, they prefer sex typical courses in teaching, fashion designing, nursing, medicine, office secretaryship and the like. The choice of institution for women is also different from men. Women are generally sent to institutions nearest to their residence though these institutions might not be rated high. We observe in our survey that nowadays we are pursuing higher and technical education. Out of 100 respondents 66 are working and are contributing to the finance of the house, and out of these 24 are graduate and 42 possess postgraduate or other technical degrees. Percentage-wise it is seen that cent per cent of under matric are housewives and have no contribution except looking after the house; the same is the position of matriculate respondents and those possessing senior secondary certificates. We see only 9.09 per cent of graduates as housewives, 18.18 per cent are pursuing further studies and of the majority of graduates 72.33 per cent are working women. Out of the total 48 postgraduates and those possessing technical degrees 6.25 per cent women are pursuing further studies; the same percentage is of housewives and 87.5 per cent are working women.

Occupation

Income plays an important role in the social status of an individual and nature of occupation is a decidable force. The occupational status of women is also one of the most important variables to determine the socio-economic character. Many studies have shown that with the increase in urban life, increase in educational opportunities, progress of technology and industries have provided multiplication of occupation alternative. The 1999 world survey on the role of women in development brought out by the UN says that the world of work is actually mixed. On the one hand, development has opened up employment opportunities and has led to a steady increase in the female share of paid employment.[2] Education consists of methodical socialisation of the young generation. Durkheim considers education as a social institution that functionally promotes consensus and social integration in the new generation through cultivation of those personal qualities that can further prove it is a social process.[3] Literacy is the key variable in the development of the people and their awareness and participation. An educated person is more conscious of his rights as well as his duties, as a citizen of his country. Education increases the degree of participation which is the key of development. The education and training in India is contributing a steady stream of trained women for the service sector, business and industry. Education regulates, controls and influences all spheres of an individual's actions. It not only influences the behaviour of the person, but also their attitudes towards modernisation and development. Therefore, it is one of the most important socio-economic status variables having an impact on the process of development. Women's empowerment is related to many variables of modernisation such as literacy, political knowledge, empathy, innovativeness, aspiration and achievement motive.

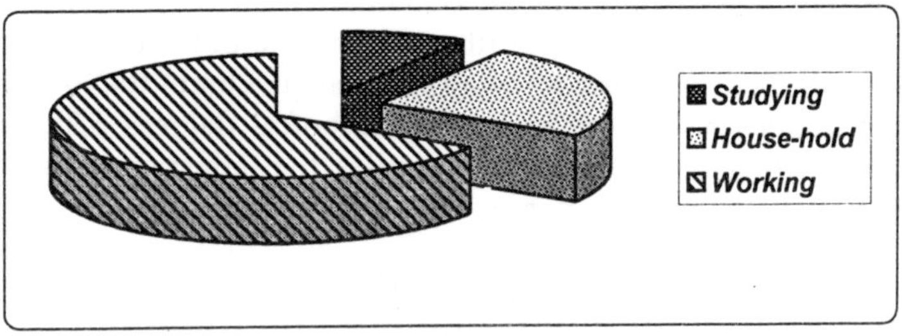

Graph 5.1: Educational Status

Technical education's contribution to human resource development is enormous particularly because of its own global spread and its own requirement of the millions of the "Knowledge Workers".

These aspects covered anti-social feeling in the mind of women against the society with different phantasies of violence and self-depression. The reason for these attitudes among the women can be rectified through comic strip mentality by giving moral training in their childhood, creating sustainability for the women development by making their wasted productive knowledge through social reforms. To raise the economical and social level of women, the government may plan policies, which can help and support them, which will be an investment in the new infrastructure, empowering them and helping them to evolve as entrepreneurs.

Table 5.3: Educational Qualification with Family Income

000's	*Under Matric*	*%*	*Matric & Senior*	*%*	*Graduate*	*%*	*PG & Technical*	*%*	*Total*
Below 5	1	14.29	-		-		6	85.71	7
%	14.28						12.5		
5 to 8	-		9	30	9	30	12	40	30
%			75		27.27		25		
8 to 15	3	7.14	-		18	42.86	21	50	42
%	42.86				54.55		43.75		
15 & above	3	14.29	3	14.29	6	28.57	9	42.85	21
%	42.86		25		18.18		18.75		
Total	7		12		33		48		100

Out of 7 respondents having a family income below Rs. 5,000, one is under matric, six possessed postgraduate or other technical degrees. Having a family income ranging Rs. 5,000 to below Rs. 8,000 out of 30 respondents nine were matric or senior certificate holder, nine were graduates and 12 were having postgraduate or other technical degrees. With a family income ranging rupees Rs. 8,000 to below Rs. 15,000 three out of 42 were under under matric, no respondent having matric or senior certificate was in this income group, 18 were having graduate degrees and half of the respondents, i.e., 21 in this income group were holding postgraduate or other technical degrees. Respondents having income above rs. 15,000, three out of 21 were under matric, three possessed matric or senior certificates, six were graduates and nine were having postgraduate or other technical degrees.

Table 5.4: Educational Qualification with Marital Status

	Under Matric	%	Matric & Senior	%	Graduate	%	PG & Technical	%	
Married	7	8.24	9	10.59	24	28.23	45	52.94	85
%	100		75		72.73		93.75		
Unmarried	-		3	20	9	60	3	20	15
%			25		27.27		6.25		
Total	7		12		33		48		100

One of the best ways of career planning even for married women is to do continuous value addition by investing in their own development. The principles of affirmative action and positive discrimination to ensure that women are properly represented in all occupations and political positions and ensure that education is available to all. Out of 85 married respondents seven (8.24%) were under matric, six (10.59%) were matric or senior certificate holders, 24 (29.23%) had completed their degree course and 45 (52.94%) were postgraduates or having other technical degrees. Out of15 married respondents three (20%) matric orsenior certificate holders, nine (60%) possessed graduate degrees and three (20%) had postgraduate or other technical degrees. Out of seven under matric all of them were married, out of 12 matric or senior certificate holders nine (75%) were married and 3 (25%) were not married. Out of 33 graduates 24 (72.73%) were married and nine (27.27%) were not married. Out of 48 postgraduate or other technical degree holders 45 (93.75%) were married and three (6.25%) were not married.

Lack of a thorough understanding between individuals of the family has also been showing correlation between breaking of joint families and indiscipline with an increase in the number of nuclear families. Value education spans the entire learning, cultivation of imagination, strengthening of will and the character. In the past, the educational process was not confronted with the different changes related with social, political and economic as it is in the present.

The value education will help young girls in becoming more capable of handling such situations. In the process, the seeds of emotional revolution are sown in every individual.

Table 5.5: Educational Qualification with Family Structure

	Under Matric	*%*	*Matric & Senior*	*%*	*Graduate*	*%*	*PG & Technical*	*%*	
Nuclear	7	12.07	9	15.52	18	31.03	24	41.38	58
%	100		75		54.55		50		
Joint	-		3	7.14	15	35.72	24	57.14	42
%			25		45.45		50		
Total	7		12		33		48		100

Education and womens rights movements have extended themselves by the force of analogy, creating the perception that different gender-biased treatments given to women were unjust, and that men and women can gain advancement only on the grounds of individual ability, and not because of the families they are lumped into. This has made for changes in family structure. Education has always been the most important part of forward movement, because it is a very important tool for doing it. Out of 58 respondents living in nuclear families seven (12.07%) were under matric, nine (15.52%) had matric or senior certificates, 18 (31.05%) were graduates and 24 (41.38%) possessed postgraduate or other technical degrees of those living in joint families none was under matric, three (7.14%) possessed matric or senior certificates, 15(35.72%) were graduates and 24(57.14%) were having postgraduate or other technical degrees. Out of seven under matric respondents cent per cent were living in families. Out of 12 respondents having matric or senior certificates 9 (75%) were living in nuclear families and 3 (25%) were in joint families. Out of 33 graduate respondents 18 (54.55%) were having nuclear families and 15 (45.45%) were in joint families. Out of 48 respondents possessing postgraduate or other technical degrees half of them in nuclear and half in joint families. One does not see much effect of family structure on the education standard of women, for women in nuclear families had a slight edge over women in joint families as far as their education is concerned.

Marital Status

The low educated group, married group and non-working group are more traditional than their respective counterpart. The married women worked out of economic necessity of improving their status, were habituated to work, and were career minded. Marriages are formal contracts by mutual agreement of both parties blessed by customs. Thė instructive desire to preserve the family's customs governs and plays an important part in the marital arrangements. Marriage is perhaps the most significant event in the life of a girl; it implies a complete break in her life. It also implies certain responsibilities on her, having a grave impact for her decision on work, employment occupation and job. Marriage coefficient point to possible productivity difference between husbands and wives are related to the traditional division of labour within the family whereby husbands tend to concentrate on income producing activities and wives concentrate on other family responsibilities.[4]

Table 5.6: Marital Status with Age Group

	20 to 30	*(%)*	*31 to 40*	*(%)*	*41 to 50*	*(%)*	*Total*
Married	16	18.82	45	52.94	24	28.24	85
(%)	57.14		93.75		100		
Unmarried	12	80	3	20	-	0	15
(%)	42.86		6.25		0		
Total	28		48		24		100

As regard the marital status of the respondents, the study found that an overwhelming majority of them were married and a few of them were unmarried. Marriage is about getting people together with give-and-take and the creation of something new. The differences between their familial practices and attitudes reflect their understanding. Out of 85 married respondents 16 (18.82%) were in the age group of 20 to 30, 45 (52.94%) were in the age group of 31 to 40 and 24 (28.24%) were in the age group of 41 to 50. Out of 15 unmarried 12 (80%) were under 30 years of age and three (20%) were in the age group of 31 to 40. Out of 28 respondents in the age group of 20 to 30, 16 (57.14%) were married. Out of 48 respondents in the age group of 31 to 40, 45 (93.75%) were married and three (6.25%) were not married. In the age group of 41 and above all the 24 respondents were married.

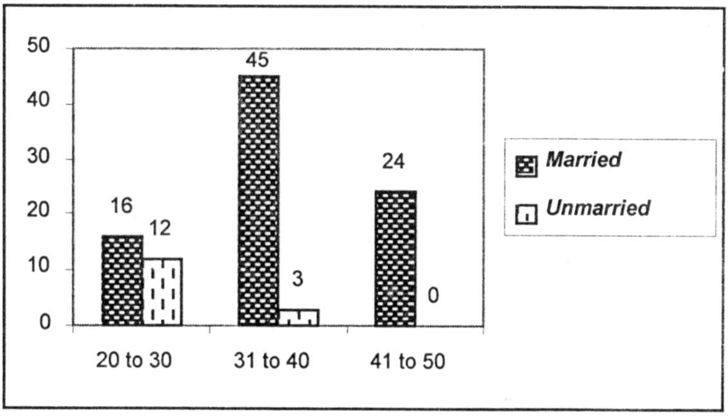

Graph 5.2: Marital & Age Scenario

Table 5.7: Marital Status with Occupation

	Student	(%)	Household	(%)	Working	(%)	Total
Married	3	3.53	22	25.88	60	70.59	85
(%)	33.33		88		90.91		
Unmarried	6	40	3	20	6	40	15
(%)	66.67		12		9.09		
Total	9		25		66		100

Women are managing two fronts: one is domestic and the other is economic. Women of the poorer section and women who are under the poverty line, are extremely overworked in both fields of earning out of the house and inhouse work. Women work harder. The problem of economic deprivation and dependency of women can only be minimised by education, and they should have to get support of all family members and the society, which will contribute to human capital formation and eliminate perpetual dependency. Out of 85 married respondents three (3.53%) were pursuing studies and were students, 22 (25.88%) were householders doing only domestic work and 60 (70.59%) were working women. Out of 15 unmarried six (40%) were students, three (20%) were household and six(40%) were working. Out of nine student respondents pursuing further studies three

(33.33%) were married and six (66.67%) were not married. Out of 25 households 22 (88%) were married and three (12%) were unmarried. Out of 66 working respondents 60 (90.91%) were married and six (9.09%) were not married.

Table 5.8: Marital Status with Family Income

000's	*Below 5*	*(%)*	*5 to 8*	*(%)*	*8 to 15*	*(%)*	*15 & above*	*(%)*	*Total*
Married	7	8.23	21	24.71	36	42.35	21	24.71	85
(%)	100		70		85.71		100		
Un-married	-		9	60	6	40			15
(%)			30		14.29				
Total	7		30		42		21		100

We have all seen the profound educational and economic shift in women that has taken place in this country as these models has begun to displace the orthodox attitudes in recent years. "Freedom depends on economic conditions even more than political. If a woman is not economically free and self-earning, she will have to depend on her husband or someone else, and dependents are never free", stated Pandit Nehru. The urge to open the field of education and economy to women were previously left out of account. One common thought is that economic ends have led to discriminated treatment to women down from generation to generation and there are many who are sympathetic with women, still regarding their economic status as pernicious. To the author economy is a matter of justice done at last. Out of 85 married respondents seven (8.23%)with family income below Rs. 5,000, 21 (24.71%) had income ranging Rs. 5,000 to from Rs. 8,000, 36 (42.35%) were in income group of Rs. 8000 to Rs. 15000 and 21 (24.71%) had income of rupees 15000 and above. Out of 15 unmarried respondents nine (60%) were in the income group of rupees 5000 to 8000 and six (40%) had income varying Rs.8000 to Rs.15000. All the seven respondents having income below RS5000 were married. In income group of Rs.5000 to Rs.8000, out of 30 respondents 21 (70%) were married and 9(30%) were unmarried. In the income group of rupees 8000 to 15000, out of 42 respondents

36 (85.71%) were married and six (14.29%) were unmarried. All 21 respondents with income of Rs. 15000 and above were married.

Structure of the Family

Family structure is a well discussed subject. Generally the difference in nuclear family and joint family is made by industrial and agricultural society. Many political scientists say that the joint family prevails and dominates agricultural society whereas the nuclear family is the fruit of industrialisation where movement, mobility, self, expression among its members is frequent. May it be nuclear or joint- family planning has a big role to play in the overall development of the family.

Table 5.9: Family Structure with Age Group

	20 to 30	*(%)*	*31 to 40*	*(%)*	*41 & Above*	*(%)*	*Total*
Nuclear	19	32.76	18	31.03	21	36.21	58
(%)	67.86		40		77.78		
Joint	9	21.43	27	64.29	6	14.28	42
(%)	32.14		60		22.22		
Total	28		45		27		100

Women should enrich themselves by retaining the traditional values and adding on the best of the modern tradition and progress. Our rich cultural heritage has thus given to our women virtues and graces that other women miss. The joint family system was favoured by majority of the respondents.

The young generation has tremendous potential to offer in the socio-economic development of the family. An analysis from the age perspective with respect to its impact on poverty, on inequality and assessment of its impact on family well-being shows that the younger generation are more likely to promote more equitable distribution of productive assets, opportunities, income and occupation. It is an interesting debate and it has to be done. Of the 58 respondents living in nuclear families, 19 (32.76%) were in age group of 20 to 30 years, 18 (31.03%) were in age group of 31 to 40 years and 21 (36.21%) were in the age group of 41 years and above. Thus at any age no women anywhere in the world should be deprived of the best education, the best teachers and the best teaching tools and aids. Education thus has become the biggest beneficiary of women in this age of information technology. Of the 42 respondents living in joint families nine (21.43%) were in age group of 20 to 30 years, 27 (64.29%) were in age group of 31 to 40 years and 6 (14.28%) were in age group of 41 years and above. Out of 28 respondents in the age group of 20 to 30 years, 19 (67.86%) lived in nuclear families and 9 (32.14%) were in joint families. In the age group of 31 to 40 years, 18(40%) out of 45 respondents were living in nuclear families and 27 (60%) were living in joint families. In the age group of 41 years and above, 21 (77.78%) were living in nuclear and six (22.22%) were living in joint families.

Table 5.10: Family Structure with Occupation

	Studying	*(%)*	*House -hold*	*(%)*	*Working*	*(%)*	*Total*
Nuclear	9	15.52	22	37.93	27	46.55	58
(%)	100		95.65		39.71		
Joint	-	0	1	2.38	41	97.62	42
(%)	0		4.35		60.29		
Total	9		23		68		100

The main aspect of the problem of working mothers and their children was that the traditional role of the women as a mother had not changed in spite of her increased educational qualifications. There is gender segregation in marketed work and domestic work. Women are mostly engaged in domestic work while men are engaged in marketed work. There is significantly a high level of segregation even in domestic activities between men and women. There are some male-dominated domestic activities like driving for family, marketing and coaching of children; the male members almost do not perform any feminine job like cooking, dusting and cleaning. Education prepares the mind to accept new roles, challenges and situation. Every man attempts to get the best job in respect of his capacity. Income plays an important role in the development of the people. While reporting the income of the respondents we have criteria in our mind that:

i) To know the source of income as the respondent is doing job working in private sector or in government job or agriculture or casual labour or studying. If he/she is studying then getting any benefit or not.

ii) To assess the income of all family members.

iii) To know how many members of the family are earning or contributing to their family income.

iv) To find out the standard of living and structure of the family.

Out of 58 respondents living in nuclear families, nine (15.52%) were pursuing studies, 22 (37.93%) were householders and 27 (46.55%)were working. Out of 42 respondents living in joint families, one (2.38%) was a householder and 41(97.62%) were working women. Each one out of nine respondents pursuing studies was living in nuclear families. Out of 23 household respondents, 22 (95.65%) were in nuclear families and one (4.35%) was living in a joint family. Out of 68 working respondents, 27 (39.71%) were living in nuclear families and 41 (60.29%) were living in joint families.

Working women coming from joint families were of the opinion that they had to share their income in order to lessen the responsibilities of male members of the family for the day-to-day needs. The women from nuclear families wanted to stay in a nuclear families for better facilities, better understanding and a place where their individuality was respected. When asked about the reason behind this they told that elder women-in-laws always used to shout at them with or without reason to make them realise their existence. They felt they did not have any feelings towards them, that they were part of the family to which they themselves belonged. Their uncompromising and unsympathetic behaviour only enhanced their authority. The view of a majority of respondents was that to make the elders in a joint family happy all the time, you have to work silently and cannot enjoy the credit of the work done by you. The concept of a joint family has not totally collapsed or vanished; in many cases, this is ineffective or socially unacceptable but changing times and the increased economic consciousness have made solutions more acceptable than traditional approaches.

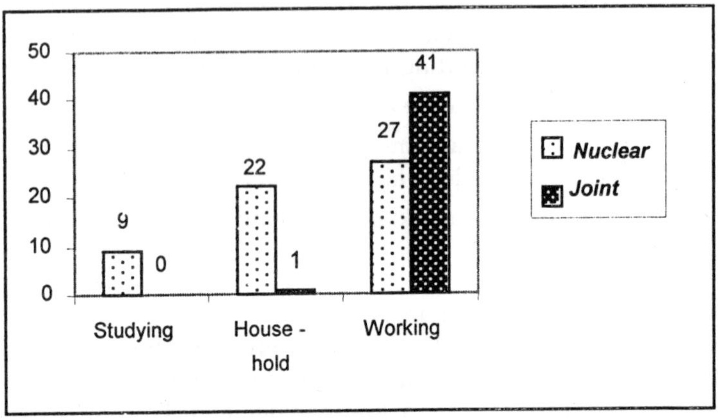

Graph 5.3: Family Structure & Occupation

The differences between mother-in-law and daughter-in-law are open secret and they work against the interests of each other. This has to be understood in the context of the changing role of education, identification and characteristics of values, their relevance and suitability in the present-day context. This has to be sensitised in societal and economic context; it has to be about development processes that constitute anthropocentric of social transformation and instrument of modern society. The higher the income of an individual, the better are his chances of coming into contact with outside world.

Table 5.11: Family Structure with Income Group

000's	*Below 5*	*(%)*	*5 to 8*	*(%)*	*8 to 15*	*(%)*	*15 & above*	*(%)*	*Total*
Nuclear	4	6.9	18	31.03	24	41.38	12	20.69	58
(%)	57.14		60		57.14		57.14		
Joint	3	7.14	12	28.57	18	42.86	9	21.43	42
(%)	42.86		40		42.86		42.86		
Total	7		30		42		21		100

Those individuals who are well placed in terms of material prosperity also have better opportunities to acquire higher education and participation in socio-political activities in the community. Out of 58 respondents living in nuclear families, four (6.9%) family income below Rs.50,000, 18 (31.03%) were in income group of Rs 5,000 to Rs. 8,000, 24 (41.38%) were in income group of Rs. 8,000 to Rs. 15,000 and 12 (20.69%) had an income above Rs. 15000. out of 42 respondents living in joint families, three (7.14%) had a family income below Rs. 5,000, 12 (28.57%) were in the income group of Rs. 5,000 to Rs. 8,000, 18 (42.86%) were in the income group of Rs. 8,000 to Rs. 15000 and 9 (21.43%) were having income of Rs. 15000 and above. Out of seven respondents having a family income below Rs. 5,000, 4 (57.14%) were living in nuclear families and three (42.86%) were in joint families; 18 (60%) out of 30 respondents in the income group of Rs. 5,000 to Rs. 8,000 were in nuclear families whereas 12 (40%) had joint families. In the income group of Rs. 8,000, Rs. 15000, out of 42 respondents, 24 (57.15%) were having nuclear families and 18 (42.86 %)were in joint families. Of the 21 respondents having income of Rs. 15,000 and above, an 12 (57.14%) were in nuclear families and 9 (42.86%) were in joint families.

Political Participation

Education plays an important role in every sphere of life, and can play an important role in development of a nation. A high percentage of literacy and education will influence political participation and awareness.[5] Literacy is universally recognised as a powerful instrument of social change. The level of literacy is undoubtedly one of the most important indicators of social, cultural and health development among the communities. Research, knowledge, organisation and administration etc. will be influenced by better and effective education. Education will help in the development of human personality, social mobility, occupational change and the rise of professional, political and social awareness. Education and high percentage of literacy will influence political participation and awareness. As Sh. Sadanand A. Shetty has written in his editorial 'One India One People', "Once education becomes compulsory and universal, people will be conscious of their rights and will not allow themselves to be exploited or treated as mere 'pawns' in the politicians game. They will, then elect their leaders on the basis of character, intellect and moral excellence rather than on the basis of caste, creed, region and religion."[6] We apply one set of standards to those outside the mainstream while the people within can do away with basic principles, especially freedom of the individual. In a democratic country everybody has equal rights. For instance, between two persons one can be rich, the other poor, one can be a Muslim, the other a Hindu, one may belong to the upper caste, the other to a lower caste; one may be a man, the other a woman. Political equality means that despite this difference both will have one vote.

Political parties play very important role in educating people and mobilising the rural folk. The political parties can play a role of right platform to give knowledge to the people, most of whom are illiterate, about their rights and duties, they can be helpful in enabling them to fully participate in the development process. Political parties should play an important role is recruiting people as their members without taking into account the religion, caste and economic status of a person. Party affiliation can be seen as one of variable of participatory attitude. The political party affiliation may have an influence on the participation of an individual in political activities.

Education-wise the respondents' affiliation with political party is 55 per cent. Membership of a political party could well be taken as an indicator of the respondents psycho-political affiliation and political attitudes. A person develops psychological identification with that political party which is closest to his / her political thinking and ideology. This psychological identification may induce him to become an active member of the political party. According to Milbrath, "Psychological identification means that the person likes the party and is inclined to support it with a vote at election time."[7] Women at the bottom of the social ladder looked towards men as their social superiors to explain the world to them. Men looked in turn to tradition and to authority in the form of various institutions, their laws and bye-laws, their interrelationships, which all are contributions of the men's ego. Education will work as the sole contributor of women's achievements, or otherwise men will drive their thoughts to wherever they want them to be. Value education would not only enhance communication but would also help women in providing effective links to other parts of the country.

The author thinks it is important to be optimistic and freedom of expression is a proof that all is not lost. Determined to give a wake-up call to the leaders will help us gauge the health of India's democracy. Women's fight is for democracy, social transformation, meaningful social justice and dignity. If any steps are taken in this regard, they will create more opportunities to expand women's ability and their personality. The debate now must be about how positive integration can ensure no one is left behind, and how we can realise the strength from our diversity as a society. So let's just stop talking about it and let us act to make sure our women are afforded a stake in politics so they feel able to value, respect and protect it.

Mass Media Exposure

While the opening up of the economy has brought growth opportunities with improved competitiveness, this has also given rise to cut-throat competition in all sectors. People have expectations of improving their life and future, and are impatient for progress. The use of electronic media, the TV and the radio is of immense importance for achieving the goal of women emancipation. During our survey we found that cent per cent of the respondents were in possession of telephone and television, 80 per cent were having cell phones, 50 per cent of the respondents were having computers and 20 per cent were having internet connection. Thus, information technology reveals a vast potential and should be aimed at improving the condition of women by analysing it in accordance with the humanitarian commitment. It is important to envision the role of this sector in any country's economy rapidly integrating into the global economic order. This implies that information technology cannot be pursued without an orientation to values. This branch of knowledge, therefore, could be expected to base itself on the ethic of humanitarianism, and to be committed first of all to the social welfare of persons. The sharp increase in systematic development of this field in terms of both quality and quantity will be helpful in the transformation of social relations and the individual life processes, which constitute them, accomplished in social interaction.

It allows exchange of information, to understand each other's issues, to build solidarity, and to have a sense that we are part of development that goes beyond the local work or the national work. As any tool, it can be really good or really bad. We need to be sure that the electronic media is responsive to women, and it can serve us for empowerment and building and for advancing women's human rights. Otherwise it can be used as a way, somehow, like mainstream media for example, where images of women are continuously portrayed to be discriminatory.

Without education there can be no progress despite their entry into the democratic process. Media must continue to monitor overall happenings and other freedom issues, and raise them as appropriate in the course of time and participate in a high-profile launch of a campaign for women's rights. Now women have a chance to learn more about them and the system. The focus must be to remove the impediments to their self-recognition: Harnessing this resource must be accepted as a challenge.

References

1. M. K. Singh, Participation of Women in Economic Development; Trends and Issues, *Indian Journal of Industrial Relations,* 1987.
2. *Times of India,* 23 Oct., 1999.
3. UNESCO: *A Dictionary of Social Science,* Edited by Julius Guide and William L. Kolb, 1964, p. 228, Quoted from *Durkheim's Education and Sociology,* Translated by S.D. Fox the Free Press, 1965, pp. 70-71.
4. T. N. Daymont and P. J Andrisan, Job Preferences, College Major and the Gender gap in Earnings, *The Journal of Human Resources,* 1984,
5. Anil Kumar Singh, *Approaches To Tribal Development,* Sarup & Sons, New Dehli, 1994, p.123.
6. Sadanand Shetty (editorial), 'No Time to Pause', *One India One People,* May, 1998, p.4.
7. Laster W. Milbrath, *Political Participation,* Chicago: Rand McNally and Co. , 1965, p. 25.

6

Women Empowerment through Education

We affirm that humans are born equal, that they are entitled to equality of opportunity, and this principle should be practised. Hope plays a big role in politics and economics, and women's education thus influences and is influenced by this thought. The road to success may appear daunting but those that are determined would be rewarded. The ability to set goals for themselves and work in a planned way towards achieving that goal are qualities which will stand our country in good stead in the future. There are lots of problems within the Indian system which need to be sorted out. It is time to revamp and rediscover these and invent new models for development.

No force in the world can make a bad person achieve stupendous success, so women can actively participate in their own becoming through education. Behaviours that are under the direct control of a person can be more effectively modified through education. A certain level of intelligence is required to manoeuvre, and attentiveness is believed to be more important than superior intelligence. We must touch on all the various aspects of society. The different Education Commissions in the past, like the Radhakrishanan Commission (1948), the Sri Prakasa Committee on Moral Instruction, the Kothari Commission (1966) Programme of Action of NPE (1992), AICTE and the Planning Commission of India have emphasized a need for the value education. Value education means a positive effect for bringing about a synthesis of physical, intellectual, emotional, aesthetic, moral and spiritual values in human beings. Education implies that a man's outlook is transformed by what he knows, where training suggests the acquisition of appropriate appraisals and habits of response in limited conventional situations, and it lacks the wider cognitive implications of education. It should be remembered that all development is self-development. By acquiring skills that are the need of the changing times, a person can enhance his value to remain relevant. To suit the present demands, women's education may be considered as:

— Development of the ability to apply knowledge for solving day-to-day problems.

— Improvement of the analytical and diagnostic skills, and development of the decision-making ability.

— Support the development of imaginative and innovative solutions to deal with real-life situations.

— To unearth their potential to work as effective team leaders, to handle tough human problems.

— To generate entrepreneurial interest and motivate themselves towards self-employment.

Education, Women and Community Betterment

Woman is the central point in the family and always works and prays for the upliftment of the family. She is the strong foundation of the house. She does not bother about her own woes, all her life serves her children without expecting anything in return. She feels great by sacrificing her interests the family. She has a great role in nation building through the development of children. In this way she always contributes towards nation building. A verse from *Rig Veda* (R.V. 160.2.6.5.1.5) states, "The sky is like a father, the earth is like mother and the space is their son. The universe consisting of the three is like a family and any kind of damage done to any of the three throws the universe out of balance." In spite of her being so important, she could not find a respectable place in society due to one reason or another. For centuries long, she has been oppressed and has been confined to the four walls of the house. She has been treated with different sets of rules. She was subjected to all type of evils such as purdah sati, etc.

Though our Constitution has granted equal status to man and woman and is not biased on the basis of gender yet the development of the woman is not up to the desired extent. Only through education and, of course, through current education woman can learn how to live in a world community. Today the world is seriously thinking to give her due respect by providing her with some extra powers so that she may live a respectful life and she may not be treated as an inferior part of society. "Perception of women in the Gram Panchayat has thus, made significant changes in their social status as well as their position within the family and village society."[1]

To some extent, the woman herself is responsible for the non-development or under-development of woman. Whenever the birth of the child takes place, it is she who first encounters the newborn child. She feels all happiness if the newborn baby is a Male and often feels disappointed if is it the opposite sex. Then during the growing period, desires to confine her daughter within the four walls of the house and she (mother) does not want her (daughter) to be exposed to the outside world. Though the time is changing very fast and she has started thinking independently and acting independently yet it is just the tip of the iceberg. A cultivation of reasoning and clarity in thinking is essential. Education must keep an eye on these areas. In the Indian context, it is said that India lives in villages and our very villages depict the very dark picture with regard to development of girls, whether in the field of education or in the grant of economic independence.

It is the need of the hour that firstly the woman herself should change her behaviour towards woman. She should feel rejoiced and there should not be hatred at the time of the birth of a girl-child. This is only the psychological feeling in the minds of parents that the son can be helpful at the time of old age. The persons who have no son can share their experience that, at times, daughter(s) usually prove to be more helpful than son(s) if she is exposed to life. Previously boys use to lend a hand in marketing, escorting their mother and sisters, but today girls are trained to do all shopping, so here again her responsibilities increase. "Increased awareness is one of the most valuable means of achieving gender equality and the girls and women's empowerment of women and girls."[2]

"Education is not a recreation club, a business concern or a gambling den. It is a social institution which should train million of our youth to face challenges, some of which are personal, some social and some related to growth and development, and all to achieve excellence in every field of human activity."[3] Education must be effective, fruitful and purposive. In this way, we may contribute towards the upliftment of women by making our own contributions for her empowerment.

Educated women should take the personal responsibility to be good citizens, and organise efforts to alert and to educate the others, but low levels of information are a reality that must be taken into account. It is unrealistic to expect everyone to have a detailed knowledge of a wide range of political matters. Besides theses characteristics, they are also affected by their own organic systems, such as physical deficiencies, an emotional disturbance and poor socio-economic conditions which affect the conduct of women as a crises in a community's physical and mental health. Education plays an important role for ensuring mobility in society and is one of the major contributors towards the progress of mankind.

EDUCATION, WOMEN AND SOCIETY

"Aurat" as a woman is called in this part of the world is a Persian word which means someone precious enough to be kept tenderly and protected. Accordingly the woman deserves a special place in society and should be considered precious. "The Indian Constitution as a living social document is not a strait-jacket and cannot be static, passive or negative. Rather it is dynamic and positive and is intended to bring about a new social order through the instrumentality of law."[4]

Even today, in spite of independence, in spite of good legislation, in spite of education of women and reduction of illiteracy, many social evils and customs exist in Indian society. Indian women on the whole never sought to sublimate or rationalise her limitation and disabilities or bypass family life. On the contrary, their homes and families have invariably come first in their order of priority. Education is expected to bring in all-round personality development in a woman, providing them with a new vision and worldview, helping her to adjust herself to the needs of her family and the community. This has the very important result, however, of maintaining a stable and integrated society.

Menfolk have devised plans to bring women on an equal footing as also to give her the desired status in society. The government has made plans to this effect, the NGOs are also active and banks have also made out new loan schemes to provide financial help. All this is well taken and they show positive signs towards the betterment of the status of women in society. We have celebrated Women's Day, Women's Year as also the Decade. Celebration may not change the status of women in our society as these are stopgap arrangements. Society has not yet succeeded in framing the required norms or institutions to enable women to fulfil multiple roles that they are expected to play in India today. "Without qualitative expansion in education, social and other disparities cannot be done away with. At the same time in the absence of qualitative achievement, socio-cultural and economic equality cannot be sustained on a permanent basis as much as the quantitative expansion of education. Sustainability of equality can be made effective only when quality factors in education such as efficient teaching, improved methods of teaching, curriculum, textbooks, infrastructure and good schooling are given utmost importance."[5]

The only way we can actually progress in this direction is to have continual progress, beginning at the grassroots level; the intention should prove this. Men still feel chivalrous when they have a protective hand over the womenfolk. Education is a powerful force in alleviating misunderstandings, tensions and persecution arising out of variation in the people and in the culture. We must empower women through education and training to help build a 'Tension-Free Society' which is the need of the country. All over the world, there is only one demand in each and every country, viz., 'to have peace, tolerance and value-oriented living'. This can be achieved only through society and education to create a culture of caring and excellence. We have to reorient our education to integrate women's studies and curriculum. We have to make our NGO's play their role more effectively along with state departments of women and child welfare, for promoting gender awareness, particularly in rural areas, and reconstruct the curriculum in secondary and higher education level to achieve this desideratum.

There is no doubt that women occupy very important place in society because they bring about the transfer of the intellectual tradition from one generation to the next. They are expected to help in the society revolution that is taking place in our society. Their influence is everlasting and they shape the destiny of future citizens. It is for this purpose that strategy must be adopted to empower women to enable them to play their role more effectively and appropriately. Promotion of social justice, democratic freedom, equality and empowerment has to be executed by them through the practice of education by laying a firm foundation in the plastic mind of young children.

Education is an important instrument for bringing change in any social set-up. "Education will be used as an agent of basic change in the status of women. Mahatma Gandhi believed in the fact that educating a single family is equal to educating the entire family. Such a value is being actively encouraged and forcefully canvassed by the modern system of education. In order to neutralise the accumulated distortion of the past there will be a well conceived edge in favour of women. The National Education System will play a positive interventionist role in the empowerment of women. It will foster the development of new values through redesigned curricula, textbooks, training and orientation of teachers, decision-makers, administrators and active involvement of educational institutions."[6] But no educational programme can contain the whole of wisdom in itself; women will have to combat from its powers of limitation. For reduction in women's sufferings it requires the cooperation of the other members of the society. Handling their lives with care, a healing touch can alleviate the sufferings of millions of women, so they remain away from the barrenness of social empathy and live happily thereafter.

Education, Women and Poverty

To empower underprivileged rural women by providing income-generating opportunities, creating livelihoods for rural women by organising self-help groups to improve their standards of living, increasing literacy level of women and help them develop a better understanding are the aims of the government. There has to be enhanced stress on improvement of the status of Indian women through education and employment. The continuing challenge for women is to ensure that all people have the knowledge and skills necessary for continuing human and economic development and for breaking the poverty cycle. This has been possible by identifying shortcomings and taking remedial measures. The government has been sensitive to the needs of women and has formulated several policies and welfare programmes for the emancipation of women in the country through a large number of economic schemes. Women do not have an effective voice in the nation's economic planning. Scholarships and financial aid should be provided to brilliant girl-children hailing from economically poor background.

Economic Impact on Education and Women

The report of the committee on the status of women in India ("Towards Equality", December 1974) finds that the disabilities and constraints of women, which stem from socio-cultural institutions, indicates that the majority of women are still very far from enjoying the rights and opportunities guaranteed to them by the Constitution. This briefly review the present status of women, and the policies and support systems for the development of women in India. The ultimate objective of any development activity is towards bringing more peace, happiness and prosperity in a balanced manner at all levels in the society; women play a critical and multidimensional role in realising these objectives.

"Ensure women's equal access to economic resources, including land, credit, science and technology, vocational training, information, communication and markets, as a means to further the advancement and empowerment of women and girls, including through the enhancement of their capacities to enjoy the benefits of equal access to these resources, *interalia*, by means of international cooperation."[7]

There are fewer women in the paid workforce than men. The employed women have to work a longer time than men, as they also have to carry the major share of household work. While within the family men control the resources and are the main decision makers, outside, in the workforce hierarchy women's status is never equal to that of men. The majority of them are confined to low-paid, low-skilled and irregular labour processes.

Women are also discriminated in land and property rights. Most women do not have any property in their own names. They are also not allowed to share their parental property. They have to face the trauma of violence in the shape of molestation and sexual harassment. A slave cannot be an owner. Women in India has no financial freedom in majority of states / cities / houses. She has to depend on the earning of her husband. A woman, who is dependent on the earning of her husband, has to adopt some of the principles of her husband. She is not free to think / speak / act in practical life so far as major decisions are concerned. If she is independent of financial source, she has the power of money, which gives material facilities required in the modern society i.e., property, car, bank balance in her name. First of all financial freedom is a must for women empowerment.

Women constitute quite a large number of working force in industries. The unemployment rate went up between 1993-94 and 2004. Sometime we find 70 per cent of the women labour force in unorganised, rural and agriculture sectors. She has been exploited because she is ignorant and does not know the rights and the laws as given by various labour laws. Knowledge of various labour laws can prevent her exploitation in many manners. Education will facilitate women in the formation of self-help groups of women for their economic empowerment, and will help in mobilising them to challenge the gender-based social structure. The emerging awareness that women are responsible, credit-worthy citizens can go a long way with a little monetary backing. A number of savings programmes and micro-credit schemes have been launched by the government as well as non-governmental organisations to provide them with the necessary financial fillip. Our greatest resource is our manpower. Induction of women power has to be related to it. All sections of the society should get adequate power needed by them. These will help the government to establish the duties and responsibilities of women and also help in ascertaining their coordination level for further improvement. It will also help in enabling them to recognise and exploit their potential, access government schemes and integrate the society.

An educated employed woman with her natural traditional goodness and grace is the ideal woman, whom everyone envision for independent India. The growing presence and success of women in high profile and / or prestigious professions and enterprises, as well as in white collar jobs, is obvious even to the naked eye.

Education Providing Working Skill of Women

A little education helps her to realise the need of economic independence and thereby command higher wages than an illiterate girl. There is an urgent need to motivate the women folk and instil in them the confidence to enable them as entrepreneurs to fulfil their role in the economic well being. Low educational levels are found to be directly related to low level of participation among women members in economic organisations. This also creates a need among the illiterates to join in doing some vocational training centres so that, with these vocations, they can earn their living and thereby maintain a better and healthier life with better status, rights, knowledge and privileges. Our experience has shown that a multidimensional approach towards family and community betterment with emphasis on education, skill development, income generation and women's development works more effectively than laws.

This issue is best summed up by Handy when he writes: "Organisations need talented women in their core jobs, therefore, not only for reasons of social fairness, important though that is, but because many of those women will have the kinds of attitudes and attributes that the new flat flexible organisations need. If they screen out the women they will handicap their futures" (*Hindu*, 1994). "Eradication of poverty based on sustained economic growth, social development, environmental protection and social justice requires the involvement of women in economic and social development, equal opportunities and the full and equal participation of women and men as agents and beneficiaries of people-centred sustainable development."[8] The emerging awareness that women are responsible, credit worthy citizens who can go a long way with a little monetary backing, a number of savings programmes and micro-credit schemes have been launched by the government as well as non-governmental organisations to provide them with the necessary financial fillip. The representation of women in premier services has also shown a consistent increase during the period 1987-2000. in IAS, the percentage of women has gone up from 7.5 per cent in 1987 to 10.4 per cent in 2000, and in IPS from 0.9 per cent to 3.3 per cent.

Policies / Plans / Programmes & Acts Supporting the Education for Women

There is room for growth. The solution lies in enforcing the rules strictly. There is today widespread agreement that development cannot be sustainable and long lasting unless people's participation is made central to the development process. The immediate need is to improve the system, both in quality and regularity. And finally, there's no substitute for a good system. However, an effective policy and implementation can mitigate the effects on our society but we don't really monitor regularly. There should be close monitoring of implementation of various programmes launched and the continuity is achieved through and by providing reinforcement. "A large number of Indian women are slowly emerging out of a system that had oppressed and exploited them for centuries. Today they have pervaded every conceivable sector of the national activity and had made their indelible impression in various fields which have so far been considered as the exclusive rights of men. But this is only one side of the coin. In our cities and villages, majority of women still suffer from drastic inequalities, despite receiving constant attention of both planners and policy makers, their life at home and outside still remain extremely ardous and monotonous."[9]

With the launching of massive programmes by the central and state governments, there is an opportunity to develop and adopt new innovative programmes for women and other economical weaker section of the society. Suffering due to social ill treatment through centuries touch all aspects of our lives individually and socially. But unfortunately these policies and programmes have not been put to proper and effective use to caution the women population so as to migrate the devastating effects of social backwardness. It is our belief that if these programmes are strictly implemented and maintained irrespective of marginally higher maintenance cost, it would save us lots of additional expenditure that is required to lay a new foundation for a progressive and just society. I don't have a negative view, but we hope future steps be taken more seriously and carefully. Any programme that intends to empower women must take into account education and other areas of life where they are not empowered or weak. It should be determined by the government to carry out a nationwide programme of education that will bring home the realisation that freedom cannot be won for any one section or for the people as a whole as long as women are kept in bondage.

The government made a number of efforts to raise the status of women. It enacted legislations to improve the condition of women and provide better opportunities for their development. There were the main acts passed by the government.

According to the Indian Contract Act, "A married woman can enter into contracts, acquire and sell property and land or borrow money."

Unmarried / married women can also take loan / overdraft from bank. It is clear that the husband will not be responsible for any transaction or debt account of his wife. A married woman can open a joint account with her husband.

1955: The Hindu Code Bill

1961: The Dowry (Prohibition) Act

1961: The Maternity Benefits Act

1971: M.T.P. (legalising of abortion)

1976: Equal Remuneration Act

1986: The Child Labour (The Prohibition and Regulation Act).

National Policy for the Empowerment of Women, 2001 India

The Development of Women and Child Department of the Indian Government evolved a comprehensive policy in 2001, aiming at empowering women towards social justice, gender equality, developing capabilities, including those related to professional, science and technology and entrepreneurship. It highlights areas such as education, health, nutrition, legal system, institutional mechanism, resource management, panchayati raj institutions, etc., which can enable women in all walks of life. The policy specially includes a comprehensive support in terms of labour legislation, social security and other services to participate in various industrial sectors such as electronic, information technology, food processing, agro-industry and textiles. The government has already announced that women can now work during night shifts in factories, for which social security and transportation arrangements are to be adequately provided. Several institutional mechanisms at the state and national levels have been set up for the development of women.[10]

Education and Reservation: Giving Safety, Security in Society

For quite some time, we are hearing of 33 per cent reservation for women in different spheres like political / education / employment fronts. At the panchayati raj level, the government has already made amendments and the women have been given 33 per cent reservation at the panchayat level. The bill for providing 33 per cent reservation to women in parliament is pending for quite some time and sincere efforts for passing the same and making constitutional amendments are required. Efforts are being a made to bring consensus among all the political parties to enact the law ensuring 33 per cent reservation for women in Lok Sabha and state assembly so as to have better participation of women in the political field. We have a great responsibility to help bring peace to our people. Humanitarian issues should not be intertwined with deep and chronic political problems. If we see change both in tone and behaviour then a new situation will develop. Whatever steps are taken should be from the perspective of social upliftment.

In the education field since the year 2000, Maharashtra has implemented the rule of 30 per cent reservation for women in colleges and professional institutions to provide impetus to give education to them. Such a step is also required to be taken for other states for upliftment of the women.

"The women who are new elite in the participatory process scenario are very much ignorant about their rights and the powers given by the Constitution of India. The performance of a person is affected by his mental status. Women's mental health was affected by the social status provided by the society, an oppressive attitude towards women by the society, discriminatory, disempowering, and restrictive attitude of society towards women were the factors which had affected their mental level and decision making. With reservation and other efforts have helped women to get rid of this human bondage."[11]

Education and Political Party: Encouraging Women

The expectations of people have risen high and are being considered as a measure of good governance. An active programme will indicate the activity and areas where the process inefficiencies occur. Using an analysis helps catalyse much towards leadership. The success of leadership can be demonstrated by implementing an activity-based system with the focus of identifying process inefficiencies. It reflects core issues such as decision making capabilities and alignment of strategic goals with operational efficiency. These are hard facts that need to be understood in the most relevant perspective for a system to be effective; rather it includes strategic issues including capacity planning and utilisation.

Leaders need to think big and should have a passion for extraordinary achievements. It needs expertise and imaginative thinking, which comes from knowledge and interest in diverse disciplines as economics, psychology, demography, ecology, sociology, geography, law, forestry, anthropology, politics, health science, fatigue dynamics, ethics, arts and many more.

Equality of women means that women should be given equal opportunity as men regarding health care, education, work participation and above all decision-making with seats in parliament, state assemblies and local level government. Efforts are being made to bring a consensus among all the political parties to enact the law ensuring 33 per cent reservation for women in Lok Sabha and state assembly so as to have better participation of women in the political field. Ashok Celly has rightly asserted, "Women's participation in political is necessary for holistic development. Women are bound to have a better perspective on vital issues such as environmental, health care and education, particularly of the girl child, as these affect them directly."One of the important obstacles for women panchayat members' participation in politics is that the women have to shoulder greater responsibilities than men in bringing up children and looking after household work. Negligence of household duties may even result in the break-up of families, and a political woman has to be cautious enough in striking a good balance between her role as a housewife and a politician.[12] Women should have the same time as men to fulfil their ambition.

Women in Panchayats: Better Equipped to take on Challenges

It is a well-known fact that gram panchayats had been in existence in ancient India, administering justice, looking after affairs of the villages and promoting community life. Panchayati raj system in India is inevitable.

Under the British rule centralising the whole power destroyed this ancient culture. Mahatma Gandhi was a strong supporter of the Panchayat system. It was Gandhi who for the first time in the twentieth century wished to revive the panchayati raj institutions with democratic basis of their own and invest them with adequate powers so that the villagers could have a real sense of 'Swaraj'. Gandhi's dream of Purna Swaraj, as he thought, could be achieved only by decentralising the power to panchayats through the panchayati raj system.

Due to deep roots of the panchayati raj system British rulers failed in every effort to wipe out this ancient institution. With the struggle for independence rural development was given a new emphasis. In 1910 the demand for the establishment of village panchayats was put forth in the Twenty Fifth session of All India National Congress. So in the 1920's in every province Panchayat acts were passed. But under these acts representatives were not elected but nominated by the government. In 1932 Gandhiji started many projects for self-reliance for the villages.

According to Gandhiji, "Democracy must in essence mean the art and science of mobilising the entire physical, economic and spiritual resources of all the various sections of the people in the service of the common good of all." His concept of panchayati raj can be explained in the least words of Thoreau Maxim,"That government is the best which governs the least."

The panchayat of Gandhiji's dream was supposed to attend to village sanitation, education, medical care, removal of social and economic disabilities and the likes. After the death of Gandhiji our leadership wanted his dream to be fulfilled and for this a community development programme was started in 1952. But this programme could not come up to the expectations due to non-participation and absence of active involvement of the local people because all the policies, plans, programmes and schemes for the local people came from government officials. Social policies aimed at the rural poor were wasteful and did not deliver the desired services to most of them. It is a well-known fact that wherever there has been a community participation and involvement, programmes have been more successful.

At any time when individuals or organisations or political parties had offered any alternative to community development programme it has been democracy at the grassroots level, i.e., micro level participation, which is panchayati raj institution. It was Gandhiji who for the first time in the twentieth century wished to revive the panchayati raj institutions with a democratic basis of their own and invest them with adequate powers so that the villagers could have a real sense of 'Swaraj'. The 73rd Amendment constitutes the PRIs as self-governing institutions, and as the third tier in the federal structure of India. The Constitution 73rd Amendment essentially lays down certain ground rules with basic structural framework so that it can withstand external interference and establish themselves as an effective and strong people's institution.

In India roots of panchayati raj are very deep. Panchayati raj institutions in India are the prime instruments of decentralisation at the grassroots level. One of the important principles of democracy is that one should not feel powerless or feel that he cannot do much to change his situation. But he should feel that he is able to influence events and process surrounding him. We must see and analyse the panchayati raj system after independence.

Poverty is the economic consequence of social backwardness and political deprivation. Participation in local administration will be helpful in enabling people below the poverty line to express and analyse the realities of their social status and economic inadequacy, evaluate by themselves their action in furtherance of their objectives. Each person is the best judge of his circumstances, and hence, he must be given an opportunity to participate in all matters concerning alleviation and elimination of the difficulties in which he is placed, such as poverty. In the word of Dr. Mahajan, "Panchayati Raj is no doubt a bold experiment in democratic decentralisation of administration. The success of such programme would depend upon the emergence of an appropriate leadership in the rural areas as well as the cooperation it is able to get from the people. As the experience of Indian economy shows Panchayati Raj has yet to go a long way before it is able to find a firm root in the soil." The importance of panchayati raj should be obvious in a country where four out of every five citizens live in the villages and where the incidence of poverty is much higher than in towns. Thoughts on rural local government or panchayati raj are thus an integral part of the concern for social and economic amelioration of the rural people.

The PRIs in India have travelled a long way to acquire constitutional recognition from a mere mentioning of it in the Constitution in the form of Directive Principles of State Policy (Article 40). It is envisaged in Article 40 that "the state shall take steps to recognise village panchayats and endow them with such power and authority as may be necessary to enable them to function as unit of self-government." This Article got a mere lip service for many years before finding a place of some importance in the form of the Balwantrai Mehta Study Team Report in 1959. In January 1957, the Balwantrai Mehta Committee was appointed to study and report the finding on community development programmes based on economy, efficiency and the extent to which the movement used local leadership.

The Government of India observed in the Third Year Plan, "The primary objective of Panchayati Raj is to enable the people of each area to achieve intensive and continuous development in the interest of the entire population. The elected representatives should be encouraged to evaluate the development of Panchayati Raj as offering new avenues of service to the people rather than the opportunities for the exercise of authority. The concept of Panchayati Raj is not limited to the non-official and democratic organisation associated with it. Representing as it does a distinct level of responsibility of functions within the general schemes of administration, Panchayati Raj comprehends both the democratic institutions and the extension services through which development programmes are executed."[13]

In order to remove the shortcomings of community development programmes such as lack of involvement of local people in the project and wastage of public expenditure, the Committee recommended that the entire rural development work should be entrusted to the elected member at the village, the block and the district level. This three-tier democratic decentralisation was given the name of Panchayati Raj, which was also a tribute to Mahatma Gandhi. Thus, on the recommendation of the Balwantrai Mehta Committee on October (Gandhiji's Birthday) 1959, panchayati raj movement was launched.

The introduction of panchayati raj system in the country is no doubt a very bold experiment. Rajasthan became the first state to pass the Panchayat Samiti and Zila Parishad Act on 2 Oct. 1959. Pandit Jawaharlal Nehru, then Prime Minister, inaugurated the panchayati raj at Nagore and later at Shadnagar (Andhra Pradesh) in October 1959. He praised the pioneering efforts of these two states in taking the most revolutionary and historic steps.

The focus of the present study is on political empowerment of women. Empowerment implies giving women the capacity to influence the decision-making process by integrating them into our political system. Implementation of this is the policy of reservation. Reserving seats for women in the political institution will provide them an opportunity to raise their grievances, and other related social and economic problems in a formal manner. This is necessary in order to ensure a better position for women in all spheres of life.

The fundamental principle of democracy is political equality, the idea that each person carries the same weight in political decision making. We would react in this way because equality of citizenship has always been central to the democratic ideal. Democracy is a way of making decision in which each person has one and only one voice. It means people deliberate about their common problems and concerns as equal. Any other arrangement would violate our belief in the intrinsic worth of individual and would fail to ensure that the government would pay equal attention to the values and interests of all citizens.[14]

Power is a wider term, which includes political, economic and other variation. It is simply the probability that man will act as another man wishes. While defining power Max Weber observes, "Power is the probability that one actor within a social relationship will be in a position to carry out his own will despite resistence."[15] With the establishment of PRIs, the people at the village level are entrusted with the power to participate freely in the process of their growth and development. According to Indira Gandhi, panchayats are formed by the people of the villages, so the control should be in their hands. We should understand that panchayats are a combination of all kinds of powers of the village people.[16]

Political participation is the backbone of a democratic system. Participation can only exist where people have a common interest. According to Riggs, "Increasing participation or involvement of the citizens in state activities, in power calculations and consequences is the process of politicisation of any state or country."[17]

According to many thinkers participation is essential for mass mobilisation in the theory of political development. Huntington said, "Modernisation means mass mobilisation, mass mobilisation means increased political participation; and increased political participation is the key element of political development."[18] Political participation's characteristics are further explained in definitions given by some thinkers, "Participation includes people's involvement in the decisionmaking process, in implementing programmes, sharing in the benefits of development programmes, and thus involvement in efforts to evaluate such programmes."[19]

The level of the participation of women in political life is an issue of concern. This is because achievement of equality in all areas is seen as inseparable from active political participation. Here political participation includes the right to vote, the right to contest, the right to candidacy, women as campaigners, women as members, women involvement in the decision-making process and appointment of women at all levels of government, including the participation of women at the grassroots through the panchayati raj institutions. The development programmes are channelled through the panchayati raj institutions. In this regard, the study seeks to answer certain questions like. Are the women aware of these programmes? If they are aware of these, to what extent have they been benefited? If benefited, which category of women benefited?

Development of masses of rural areas depends upon the motivation, awareness, literacy, health and knowledge about the programmes formulated by the government for their upliftment. The government since independence has been working on this but the panchayati raj system can play the more important role in the rural development. Without effective leadership at the local level and enthusiastic participation on the part of rural population the desired results cannot be achieved.

The Indian economy is undergoing a rapid transformation, from one of the stagnant and morbid economies to one of the most vibrant, progressive and challenging economies of the world with very little transparency. Population growth, illiteracy, malnutrition, basic health care, and poverty levels continue to be the areas of concern and at the same time, the veracity of our governance, political will, accountability and ethical practices are yet to be established. For the sake of maximisation of personal gains, the leaders and political parties cannot or should not forget their responsibilities towards the society in which they are operating, and need to understand that the vast majority of rural India does not need charitable hospitals, free schools, free mid-day meals or free energy and water. They rather require ways and means to alleviate their poverty through sustainable measures or build their capacity to afford a decent standard of living leading to growth of the society.

Millions of women have the potential to become part of the development process if helped, and for this the government must build sensitivities and capabilities to reach the women and the underprivileged. Women can play a lead role confidently that they could turn the fortune of the state. Capacity building of women should be treated as an investment for future growth. Every person has in him the potential to excel and all he has to do, is to create a favourable environment. There are no failures in life but there are only learning experiences, so it is suggested that training courses should be organised to improve their performance. There is lack of training of skill development and the training process not being optimum for women panchayati raj members to grow. Recycling resources through training is a way for conserving resources. The more often a skill or resource is used, the greater would be the resource leverage. These panchayati raj members need a continuous up gradation of skills, which can be done by training. There is also a challenge to provide quality service to people and thus, the strategic training programme may include training about systems, culture, etc. Training panchayati raj members on a continuous basis improves their quality and efficiency and training will bring out a drastic change in them. We should realise that change is a continuous process. Human creativity being the highest product of training, results from continuous engagement of ideas and action with the aim to learn and face challenges which are embedded in one's tasks or objectives. Training is not just a reaction to the present-day problems but is also a means to seize unique opportunities that can bring forth fundamental improvements, ability to take advantage of circumstances and snatch opportunities to meet changing environment and the ability to think in a creative way, so we can say that the notion of training can also apply to methods, techniques and new applications.

This is where leaders and political parties should visualise and plan strategies to focus on the community, society and women in the area of their operation. Changing one's lifestyle requires a great deal of effort. The wellness programme will provide a structure and climate that will encourage women to achieve what is expected from them. Personal commitment can only be achieved when given full authority where all specific and achievable goals are clearly written. The social responsibility of the leaders and the political parties call upon them and the government to devise well defined policies and goals so that women become self-sufficient and help the government to grow and achieve the set goals. Social responsibility is a virtue, which should be practised by our leaders, rather than look at it with contempt. Enforceability will not produce the desired results unless they themselves inculcate the idea of social responsibility as one of their visions. Unless women are made self-sufficient and the environment is made conducive to their empowerment, the day is not far behind when social disparities and depleting environment will thrust development into an irreversible situation where neither the leaders nor the political parties can bail the country's economy out.

EDUCATION AND MEDIA: MARCHING WOMEN TOWARDS EQUALITY

There is very hot talk today for the empowerment of women in every field of life whether it is parliament, state assemblies, media, corporate offices and so on. It does not mean that woman is powerless. God has created her with super power. She has given birth to all humanity and one can imagine the power of woman from this truth alone. Education plays an important role in the use of mass media and "Literacy and media participation are highly correlated."[20] Its influence and impact on communication, commerce and intellectual freedom is unprecedented. "Communication makes human social life possible. The nature and quality of our communication process mould the character of our social life."[21] Society is formed from human communication and human communication is formed by interaction. Interaction in the society is seen in the form of interaction communication, group communication and forms of mass media. Interaction between one man to other is the base of social life. This interaction communication is evident in traditional society, whereas in modern society tangible communication is more prevalent. "No modern society functions efficiently without a developed system of mass media."[22]

The scenario is fast changing with the advent of new and fast medium of communication. Women are getting more freedom and access to new gadgets. Now, we have the television in every home and the era of computerisation is growing fast. Internet has become the order of the day, which provides global interaction. Days are passing by when the menfolk were holding larger share of TV time in the serial and soaps. The women hold the key to success of soaps and serials at prime time and most of the women characters are shown working outside the home, having strong personalities and striving for independent identities.

New means of communication are bringing revolutionary changes in the social thinking and ideological outlooks. Mass media of communication can also act as catalytic agents in developing achievement mobility and scientific orientations. Whether one looks at the traditional media institutions of press, radio and television, or the newly emerging sectors of telecommunications, multimedia and e-media, the picture is similar. There have been some encouraging developments, which can be attributed in part to the growing maturity of the women's movement. Interaction and dialogue between gender specialists and media professionals has proven an innovative and often successful strategic approach in the struggle to change. The mass media are a powerful means of education. As an educational tool the mass media can be an instrument for educators and governmental and non-governmental institutions for the advancement of women and for development. Computerised education and information systems are increasingly becoming an important element in learning and the dissemination of knowledge. Television especially has the greatest impact on young people and, as such, has the ability to shape values, attitudes and perceptions of women and girls in both positive and negative ways. Resources allocated to education, particularly for girls and women, are in many countries insufficient and in some cases have been further diminished, including in the context of adjustment policies and programmes. Such insufficient resource allocations have a long-term adverse effect on human development, particularly on the development of women.

Globalisation

Women continue to do their roles primarily within the family in India. Though they have now started working outside, it's more for maintaining a certain lifestyle than because of the desire to have a career. The last millennium has seen the woman evolve as a daughter, a mother, a wife and so on. Thanks to globalisation and global opportunities, there has been a paradigm shift in the various roles of the women. In the Indian context, women's participation in the management field has increased substantially in recent years. This confers recognition of competence of this previously neglected segment of workforce and makes the "women in management" issue a popular topic for discussion. But here a major question arises : is this segment still a vulnerable niche with different sets of expectations, competencies and image?

Does the issue need to be addressed separately? To delve into the present status of Indian women in management, we need to peep into their mindset and evaluate them. Let's start with the views of the stakeholders. Once we get their feedback, it will be easy to match it with the expectations of women in management, and identify the gap between their ambitions and achievements.

Globalisation can be understood and defined mainly in two ways. One is the economic, the other is the non-economic which broadly includes socio-cultural, historical and political dimension of globalisation. The economic argument of globalisation appears stronger and widespread than other aspects of cultural globalisation as is generally done in the existing literature on globalisation.

Both of these cannot be separated from each other and it is difficult to observe cultural dimension of globalisation and economic dimension of globalisation independently. In this chapter I want to take the privilege to present social or cultural perspectives of globalisation. Globalisation can be used as a tool for intensifying worldwide social relations which link distant localities in such a way those local events are shaped by events many miles distant. The social norms, cultural beliefs, and the fabric of social interaction are the main ingredients of globalisation of culture and can be spread through globalisation of knowledge. Diverse social and infrastructural needs must be addressed more or less simultaneously to ensure a nation's future growth and prosperity. It is vital to understand the role of culture and collective benefits designing better and more appropriate economic policy. Cultural globalisation will be helpful in the growing awareness that we are all part of one human family, sharing the earth as our common home as nature doesn't understand national borders. The ideal cannot be sustained unless grounded consciously, and managed adequately and appropriately.

How do we ensure global competitiveness? The answer to all such and related questions lies in strengthening first the women with education in a systematic and visionary manner. Education is the first step in ensuring that women realise their full potential and become equal partners in development. Education will not only give women the much needed confidence and equip them to face the challenges of a changing world environment due to globalisation but this will lead them towards awareness of rights, effective political participation and a better quality of life.

According to Henry Mintzberg, an expert on leadership and other management issues, "The time is long since past when women succeeded by learning to play according to men's rules. Today business needs something that women can give it." In a similar tone, Professor Judith Rosener also advocates that women make their way to the top management not by adopting the style and habits judged successful for men, but in making use of their own experience. Their success depends precisely on certain characteristics generally regarded as feminine and unsuitable for a leader. Though we often describe male managers as being directive, self-centred/self-interested, decisive, aggressive, task-oriented and female managers as being participative, collaborative, cooperative, people-oriented, caring, our study on 100 working and non-working females reveals some interesting findings. As a part of this study we try to identify the perceptions of women about their female colleagues in the workplace. To do that, we analysed their perception on different dimensions. All respondents were asked to share their feelings about their female co-workers on the basis of their positions in their work places. A close analysis of their statements tempted us enough to relate findings with their psychology on their working men and women. Initially the women feel comfortable working under a male boss. Women in junior positions start with a positive perception with a smooth journey in their working, feel a positive sense of cooperation and find themselves confident in the presence of their male boss. Whereas respondents said that you can enjoy a smooth time with your female boss until you don't ask credit for your work and she will treat it as an unfair demand. A majority were of the view that women bosses take more time to choose a way out due to some indecisive trait due to their social backwardness. How can we ensure global competitiveness and answer to such questions lie in strengthening first the faculty members of colleges and educational institutions, in a systematic and visionary manner.

Education & Human Rights: Protecting Women

Our Constitution provides for liberty, fraternity, equality and justice. It contains a number of provisions for the empowerment of women such as Article 14 provides for equality before law. Article 15 (1) provides for no discrimination by the state on the grounds of religion, race, caste, sex, and place of birth. Article 39 (a) and (d) provides for state policy for equality of men and women, and for equal pay for equal work for both men and women and Article 51 (A) (e) is there for harmony and to renounce practices derogatory to the dignity. According to Ganhiji, there should be equality for women in all spheres of life. It is insulting to regard women as weak because they possess soul-force and the spirit of self-sacrifice. Gandhiji regarded women as the apostle of non-violence; she is more trained in non-violence than man. Pandit Jawaharlal Nehru said that when women move forward, the family moves, the village moves and the nation moves.

The public debate on rape generated by the emerging women's movement in the early 1980s can, perhaps, be credited with bringing sex out of Indian closets. However, this development has also turned out to be a double-edged sword.

Swamy Vivekanand asaid, "Arise and Awake" to the women of the world for want of empowerment, and for this they could have raised their voice for "Equality, Dignity and Self."[23] The immediate future is not great unless we start turning things around. Studying a range of parameters that have a direct bearing on what would be the level of impact but which were not taken into account so far in assessing will be the guiding spirit. Thanks to the women's movement, issues such as marital rape, custodial rape (i.e., by persons with authority in public institutions), sexual harassment, sexual abuse in childhood (including incest), trafficking in and exploitation of women and children by the commercial sex trade, have been recognised and public discussed. This has enable social, legal and judicial action to deal with such abusive behaviour and situations.

However, sexual crimes against women have by no means abated. In fact, they seem to be taking on even more abhorrent forms. Take, for example, the recent cases of 'serial' or 'relay' rape in Kerala, in which teenaged girls were hoodwinked and sexually abused as they were passed on from man to man and moved from place to place in different parts of the state.

The consciousness generated by the movement has led to some public and official recognition of women's legitimate sexual rights and needs. However, at another level, this development has been exaggerated and distorted by commercial interests and turned into a superficial celebration of women's sexual liberation which amounts to little more than yet another opportunity to commercially exploit the female body.

Education is a powerful tool of empowerment in the hands of the poor and the deprived especially women. In some places, such as Andhra Pradesh, women's awakening through literacy led to spontaneous and successful campaigns against arrack (country liquor), spearheaded by poor, rural women.

The Directive Principles of State Policy contained in Part IV of the Constitution. Direct the state to protect the human rights of women including the right to equal pay for equal work, the right to health and work in hygienic conditions, the right to maternity benefit, the right to gender justice, etc. The women should use their education to recognise their status in life and to improve it by knowing and exercising their rights.

Education is a human right and an essential tool for achieving the goals of equality, development and peace. Non-discriminatory education benefits both girls and boys and thus ultimately contributes to more equal relationships between women and men. Equality of access to and attainment of educational qualifications are necessary if more women are to become agents of change. Education plays an active role in elevating women's position and promoting their rights in society. With the spread of education among women, exploitation and oppression of women will be considerably reduced. This will in turn lead to the acceptance of social values that encourage economic independence and social justice for women paving the way for mutual respect and recognition of sexes. Literacy of women is an important key to improving health, nutrition and education in the family, and to empowering women to participate in decisionmaking in society. Investing in formal and non-formal education and training for girls and women, with its exceptionally high social and economic return, has proved to be one of the best means of achieving sustainable development and economic growth that is both sustained and sustainable. Education should be promoted for the development of mankind and for the creation of an international society. International understanding is therefore the need of the day. Education is a strong and potent agency of promoting this education.

Judicial March Towards Women Empowerment

In one century women have achieved legal and legislative equality in most countries of the world. However, equality in actual fact remains a goal that has yet to be achieved. The International Women's Day is an ideal occasion to examine the progress that has been made in the promotion of gender equality and to identify the challenges that are still to be overcome. Once these challenges are identified, it then becomes possible to take action in ways that would ultimately improve the role and status of women worldwide.

Women have been regarded as the second sex through the ages but the time has come to consider whether they are really subservient to men. In ancient times, we have heard of many women who have been the rulers. We have heard about Jhansi ki Rani, Razia Sultana, etc. The women in India have always been honoured and respected. Ours is one of the few countries in the world to give the women the right to vote. Our Constitution also guarantees equal rights to men and women. It is, therefore, evident that the Indian women are equal members of society and are free to work, earn and learn. So an Indian woman, endowed with these traditional culture and values, becomes a polished diamond, on getting modern education and professional skill. The attention towards the empowerment of women in India should be given priority. If the woman is capable of doing any work, she will definitely give her child better care, education health, etc. The aim is to provide educational and vocational training primarily to girls.

On a regional level, girls and boys have achieved equal access to primary education, except in rural areas where access to education facilities is still inadequate. Progress has been made in secondary education, where equal access of girls and boys has been achieved. Enrolment of girls and women in tertiary education has increased considerably. Private schools and colleges have played an important complementary role in improving women access to education at all levels. The World Conference on Education for All in 1990 at Jomtien, Thailand adopted the World Declaration on Education for All and the Framework for Action to Meet Basic Learning Needs.

Approximately 100 million children, including at least 60 million girls, are without access to primary schooling, and more than two-thirds of the world's 960 million illiterate adults are women. The high rate of illiteracy prevailing in most developing countries remains a severe impediment to the advancement of women and to development. Discrimination in girls' access to education persists in many areas, owing to customary attitudes, early marriages and pregnancies, inadequate and gender-biased teaching and educational materials, sexual harassment and lack of adequate and physically and otherwise accessible schooling facilities. Girls undertake heavy domestic work at a very early age. Girls and young women are expected to manage both educational and domestic responsibilities, often resulting in poor scholastic performance and early dropout from the educational system. This has long-lasting consequences on all aspects of women's lives.

The creation of an educational and social environment, in which women and men, girls and boys, are treated equally and encouraged to achieve their full potential, respecting their freedom of thought, conscience, religion and belief, and where educational resources promote non-stereotyped images of women and men, would be effective in the elimination of the causes of discrimination against women and inequalities between women and men. Women should be enabled to benefit from an ongoing acquisition of knowledge and skills beyond those acquired during youth. This concept of lifelong learning includes knowledge and skills gained in formal education and training, as well as learning that occurs in informal ways, including volunteer activity, unremunerated work and traditional knowledge.

The science curricula in particular are gender-biased. Girls are often deprived of basic education in mathematics and science and technical training, which provide knowledge they could apply to improve their daily lives and enhance their employment opportunities. Advanced study in science and technology prepares women to take an active role in the technological and industrial development of their countries, thus necessitating a diverse approach to vocational and technical training. Technology is rapidly changing the world and has also affected the developing countries. It is essential that women not only benefit from technology, but also participate in the process from the design to the application, monitoring and evaluation stages. To address inequality in access to educational opportunities, governments and other organisations should promote an active and visible policy of mainstreaming a gender perspective into all policies and programmes, so that, before decisions are taken, an analysis is made of the effects on women and men. An equal access to education by taking measures to eliminate discrimination in education at all levels on the basis of gender, race, language, religion, national origin, age or disability, or any other form of discrimination should be the goal of the government.

The government should also adopt a positive appropriate action plan to eliminate gender disparities in all areas of tertiary education by ensuring that women have equal access to career development, training, scholarships and fellowships. Parents, non-governmental organisations, including women welfare organisations, communities and the private sector, young women with academic and technical training, career planning, leadership and social skills and work experience should come forward to prepare women to participate fully in society. To widen girls' future career opportunities non-discriminatory and gender-sensitive professional school counselling and career education programmes to encourage girls to pursue academic and technical curricula should be taken on a war footing.

Gender inequality has been the oldest problem ever since Adam and Eve came into being. Women have been described as fairer and weaker sex in common phrases all over the world. Lack of education, lack of opportunity in employment, least participation in decision making and nutritional stress are the common characteristics of a typical woman across the globe. The difference is only in degree and magnitude. In India in spite of every grim looking scenario, women have by and large always been honoured and respected. It believed that no Yagya can be performed without the presence of women. Stories from mythology even show that a person was recognised with the name of his mother rather than father. Ours was among the first few countries to give women the right to vote.

Women have always been given a privileged status in law. Be it criminal law, constitutional law or family law, women have always found favour from Indian Law makers. It was always believed that women need to be given special status so as to ensure its upliftment and prosperity which would bring prosperity for the whole society. The concept of women empowerment is enshrined in the Indian Constitution in its Preamble, Fundamental Rights, Fundamental Duties and Directive Principles. The Constitution of India, the largest constitution in the world, the most beautiful document of the present times, commits to secure all the people justice—social, economic and political, equality of status, opportunity and before the law, freedom of thought, expression, belief, faith, worship, vocation, association and action subject to law and public morality. It ensures liberty, fraternity, equality and justice. The number of articles of Indian Constitution guarantee greater freedom for women empowerment. It recognises women's right to equality and non-discrimination. As regards the Indian Constitution, it guarantees not only the equality before law and equal protection of law to women but also confers certain affirmative rights. Our Constitution also provides for liberty, fraternity, equality and justice. It contains a number of provisions for the empowerment of women such as the following.

Article 14 : Equality before Law

Article 15(1) provides for no discrimination by the state on the grounds of religion, race, caste, sex and place of birth.

Article 15 (3) makes it mandatory for the state to make special provision for women and children. Consequently, the state has introduced reservations for women in public employment, in admissions to educational institutions and the legislatures at least at the local self government level, among other schemes for their benefit.

Article 16 envisages equality of opportunity in the matters relating to employment or appointment in any office under the state and thus give equal status to women or workplace and in the matter of seeking empowerment.

Article 39 (a) speaks out about state policy to be directed to securing the right to an adequate means of livelihood for men and women.

Article 39 (d) guarantees non-discrimination in payment of salary and wages for women on the principle of equal pay for equal work, irrespective of sex.

Article 42 requires state to make provisions for securing just and humane condition of work and for maternity relief.

The Maternity Benefit Act is a special enactment for women which ensures special leave, special conditions at workplace and nature of job to be performed during the period of pregnancy of women employees.

Article 51 (A) (e) ensures to promote harmony and to renounce practices derogatory to the dignity of the women.

Even the Fundamental Duties contained in part IV-A of the Constitution also enshrine the principle of dignity.

Thus the Indian Constitution not only guarantees equal status to women in society but also ensures and directs the state to make special laws for women on various subjects.

The Indian Penal Code lists out various offences against women and ensures that due justice should received by aggrieved women and provides for exemplary deterrent punishment for the guilty. Few of the very important provisions are Sec. 304 (B) relating to dowry death, Sections 312 to 316 for causing miscarriage, Sec. 354 assault or criminal force to women with intent to outrage her modesty. Sec. 375 and 376 deal with rape. Besides these, two whole chapters containing Sec. 490 to 498 are devoted to offences relating to marriage. Sec. 498 (A), a very important section, deals with cruelty against women by husband or his relatives, Sec. 509 deals with offences involving acts intended to insult the modesty of a woman.

Thus, the Indian Criminal Law guarantees safety to women against marital crimes, physical crimes and crimes against her modesty. However, the Indian Criminal Law does not recognise marital rape which has been accepted as crime in various other advanced countries.

The Indian Succession Act 1956 provides equal right to women to inherit property from her father as well as from her father-in-law if she becomes widow. This was the first major step after independence which broke the traditional barrier of male dominance of succession. The Indian Succession Act gave much desired attention to inheritance by women. It is evident from the fact that the list of Class 1 legal heirs contains eight female relationships out of the total twelve relationships. It makes mother a Class 1 legal heir but the father does not find place among the list of Class 1 legal heirs.

The Indian Marriage Act 1955 was also directed to strengthen the rights of the women in matrimony. It gave additional grounds for women to seek divorce. The right against marital cruelty, against conversion of husband, incapacity to perform sex were made as additional grounds to seek nullity to matrimonial relationship. The Civil Procedure Code provides alimony from the husband, thus making her financially sound even when separated from husband.

Not only and the women benefit through the enactment of laws but Indian women found favour from the judiciary also. In various landmarks judgments delivered by courts in India, the rights of women have been recognised. In a landmark judgment in 1997, the Supreme Court of India took a strong stand against sexual harassment of women in the workplace. It was made mandatory for every organisation to set up a mechanism for prevention and redressal of sexual harassment cases.

At the time of the 1981 Census it was felt that the contribution of women in the field of agriculture was not being properly recorded, and therefore a distinction was made between a main worker and a marginal worker, so as to include the contribution of women who were involved in seasonal activities in agriculture. In the year 2001 another dimension was added to it, and special efforts were made to identify and enumerate women workers in agriculture which were invisible in their previous census. However, women and girls doing domestic work in their own homes including collection of water, fuel and fodder, cooking, cleaning and care of children continue to be invisible in the 2001 Census.

REFERENCES

1. Bhola Nath Gosh, *Rural Women Leadership,* Mohit Publications, New Delhi, 2002, p. 104.
2. Beijing Declaration.
3. *Social Action*, vol. 52, No. 4, Oct.-Dec., 2002, p.366.
4. D. K. Batt, *Human Rights and Status of Women: A Socio-Legal Analysis,* A. I. R. 2000 (journal section), p. 79.
5. *Social Action*, op. cit., p.369.
6. *National Policy on Education*, 1986.
7. Declaration, op. cit..
8. Ibid.
9. H. C. Upadhyay, *Status Women in India,* Anmol Publications Pvt. Ltd. New Delhi. 1997, p. 113.
10. *National Policy for the Employment of Women, 2001-India,* Department of Women and Child Development
11. Jasprit Kaur Soni, *Introspection of Tribal Development*, Sonali Publications, New Delhi, 2004, p.182.
12. Bhola Nath Gosh, op.cit., p.100.
13. Government of India, *Third Five Year Plan Planning Commission,* New Delhi, p. 338.
14. Edward S. Greenberg & Benjamin I. Page, *The Struggle for Democracy,* Wesley Educational Publishers Inc. United States, 1999, p.10.
15. Weber Max, *The Theory of Social and Economic Organisation,* Oxford University Press, New York, 1947, p.147.
16. Manoj Sharma, *Rajasthan Vikas,* April-July, 2001, p. 8.
17. F.W. Riggs, *Bureaucracy and Political Development* Princeton, N. Univ. Press, 1963, p. 139.
18. Samuel P. Huntington, Political Development and Political Decay, *World Politics*, Vol. XVIII, No.3, April 1963, p. 388.
19. Uphoff N. T. and Cohen, J, *Feasibility and Application of Rural Development Participation: A State of the Art Paper,* Cornell University, U.S.A., 1979.

20. Danial Learner, *The Passing of Traditional Society: Modernising the Middle East*, The Free Press, New York, 1968, p.57.
21. Paul B. Horton, Gerald R. Leslie, *The Sociology of Social Problems*, Princeton-Hall, Inc., United States of America, 1978, p. 482.
22. Danial Learner, op.cit., p. 55.
23. *Review of Politics*, Vol. XIV, No. 1, Jan.-June, 2006, p.50.

7

Hindrance in Women's Arising and Awakening

A Brief

Women, from time immemorial, especially in our society, have been ill-treated and discriminated. They enjoy good position in some societies but their overall position everywhere is lower than their male counterpart. "Our women have more right than women of other countries, but there are large areas wherein women are suffering, where, may be they are not conscious of their rights."[1] Since independence lots of changes have been observed in the status of women, but their exploitation is still at an alarming state. Inequalities, sexual discrimination, violence are still stopping women in coming forward, the result of which is gross human rights violation of women every day. Women in India have many disabilities like women in the other parts of the world and experience more extensive discrimination in this sex segregated society; this is all due to lack of education.

Women have been subjected to neglect, discrimination, child sexual abuse, incest, harassment for dowry, physical battering, verbal and emotional abuse, psychological torture, marital rape, etc. The home and family, many women argue, have hardly ever been safe spaces for them. When people have the habit of generalising a person on gender basis this is all about a person's life shaped by the social position given by the society to the person. The psychological aspects are many, which constitute a person's behaviour, his habits, lack of education and indiscipline. Since the human factor is responsible for the great majority of crimes against women, behavioural modification is an important strategy. This is an eye opener for the policy makers who have forgotten the issues of the disabled totally but also attempts to remind them of their responsibilities.

Guru Nanak, who started Sikh religion, and later all Sikh Gurus strongly and firmly showed their concern and raised their voices to uplift the women thereby empowering them, initially by giving them due respect in the society. In *Guru Granth Sahib* page 473, Sri Guru Nanak says: "In a woman, man is conceived, from a woman he is born, with a woman he contracts friendship; why denounce her, or from whom kings are born?" The new race of men started regarding women as equal partners in the great task of social and national reconstruction. Female education is spreading rather rapidly.[2] Indian women in the aggregate have a low status by measurable development indicators, such as income, employment, health, and education. There are many women in visible positions of power and prestige. This situation is less paradoxical when viewed against the historical circumstances that have resulted in women in some sections of the populace gaining advantages.

In the nineteenth century, men who were exposed to Western education and liberal ideas turned a critical eye on their own society. One of their major concerns was the position of women in Hindu society. Through legislation and stirring public opinion, they sought to remove such evil practices as child marriage, sati, and the cruel treatment of widows. These social reformers saw education as the main instrument of women's emancipation.[3]

Making people believe is the ultimate success for any programe. A desire for leading rather than following have a view on how to make human conditions and environment just a little better and work towards making it happen. After years of oblivion and drawing solace only from each other's miseries education will help women by transforming them into real believers. Honesty, hard work and integrity along with consistent efforts are the essential requirements to achieve success. Education should be seen as the knowledge of the entire field of life, and must provide opportunities for the full development of the mental, moral, spiritual and physical attributes of women.

There is a need to understand how today's woman is different from her predecessors. But these women have not had it so easy;

their path was not strewn with roses. They have not realised their goals by mere luck. They have struggled harder than their male counterparts to reach the coveted positions they now occupy. Unfortunately, somehow the male ego does not allow men to accept women in higher positions, guiding them, showing them what to do and how to do. But rigid societal rules, which do not give women the freedom they require, are still prevalent.

Low Educational Level

During our field survey questions were asked about the education facilities. There were answers which gave the full picture of the education, some of them told about the facilities provided by the government, non-availability of teachers. Some of them were more elaborate and said that the government is laying more stress on adult literacy whereas it should provide more infrastructure and other facilities to attract and educate the children who are the future of our nation. These views seem to be the reflection of the *National Sample Survey*, "Literacy is an attribute which a persons generally acquires during childhood. Children who miss the opportunity of becoming literate at school going ages generally remain illiterate throughout their life. The current stock of literate population in a society is the aggregate of literate persons in different age cohorts and the size of the stock is the outcome of the extent of participation of those cohorts in education to become literate at their childhood. Thus the rate of literacy among older cohorts would by and large indicate the extent of participation in earlier years while that among younger ages would be a reflection of the more recent experience. The child literacy rate for any cohort of population is steadily increasing over time. Thus, proportionately larger number of literate population is being added to the stock while depletion due to death, generally at older ages, reduce a proportionately much smaller number of literate persons. Therefore, the more literacy among children, the larger will be the stock and if a higher literacy rate for children is maintained over a long period, the literacy level of the total population will consequently tend to rise to a higher level. Hence, there should be some relationship between the overall literacy rate and the rate of literacy among children."[4] The stress is on : All children in school by 2003; all children to complete five years of schooling by 2007; reduction of gender gaps in literacy and wage rate by at least 50 per cent by 2007.[5]

Low educational levels are found to be directly related to low level of participation among women. Women are unable to take decisions and improve their style of work, and are rarely shown as capable professionals. Women's education in India has not received due attention by the government, NGO's and the researchers in the field of education. There was general willingness in a majority of respondents to spend money for the daughter's education but they feel handicapped due to constant domestic difficulties. Women often see themselves as being at war with the existing order of things. These dilemmas can be resolved by addressing the problems in a holistic manner.

Defective Education System

Education for women at the primary and higher stages is still an imitation of boys' education. The enrolment of girls for vocational and special education is still not impressive. Some facilities are being provided to educational institutions but they are inadequate. The special courses for women like home science, drawing, painting, music, nursing etc. still need improvement. Much emphasis is now being laid on physical education of women. Funds for women's education are available but proper utilisation is needed.[6] Women's education at present, the progress made since independence in the higher system of education, is yet revealing. As such, today there are more than 1,200 institutions (out of 9,200) for women in different disciplines. Institutions for women no doubt cater to interested women, but a large number of them still do not get entry into the higher education, because of the limited opportunities and facilities.[7] Woman is not in the mainstream of education and the gender gap in access to education is a major obstacle to women's development.

When asked about the standard of education in India their views in this regard were explicit. Expansion of low grade educational system after independence has been producing degree holders who lack any behavioural knowledge and moral etiquette. The education system is degree-oriented, not employment-oriented. It lacks technical and entrepreneurial know-how for self-employment. Today education has become an alternative to employment. Students go on doing B.A., M.A. or Ph. D. till they get any gainful employment due to the present education system which has ignored its true aim of strengthening the fundamental aspiration of women. As a result injustice, illiteracy, economic inequality, erosion of ethical and moral values are getting accelerated in society. A handful of colleges are good, but the vast majorities are not. Based on the Indian ethos and the economic realities, some values to be exhibited by teachers and to be included in the educational programme are the social way of thinking, excellence in work, courage in leadership and integration. To carry out such an important responsibility, our leaders, teachers and officials need strong values in their own life and inculcate it in the future generation.

When asked about education cent per cent of the respondents said that it means not the amplification of a knowledge, which was up till now found incomplete, but the notion that what has heretofore been ignored is valuable, and what has hitherto been valued is pernicious, being the part of men's conspiracy of women oppression. The author confeses that she has met many learned personalities of recent education and social workers who knew that the new value education is a tool to perfection but were ignorant of great change and content to be the same. What is this attitude? Obviously it embodies a playing out in education of a contemporary social drama that ranges far beyond the sphere of value education of today itself.

UNEMPLOYMENT

Unemployment is a situation characterised by the existence of able persons who are willing to work but have to remain without a job. Unemployment is the clean waste of resources of a nation and threat to political and economic stability. In most countries, unemployment is one of the most serious social and economic problems of the day. It exists in an alarming degree, not only in poor countries, but also in apparently prosperous lands like England and the United States of America. In the context of countries like India the educated unemployment has turned out to be a very serious and menacing problem. A Task Force on Employment opportunities was set up by the Planning Commission under the chairmanship of Dr. Montek Singh

Ahluwalia, then member of Planning Commission. The objective was to examine the existing employment situation in India and suggest strategies of employment generation to provide jobs to 10 crore people over the next 10 years. Several academicians and bureaucrats were the member of this task force. No doubt, the rapid growth of high school and college education is a striking achievement of the Indian government, but it is also a major challenge because employment opportunities suitable to them have not expanded at the same rate.[8] On the basis of the data collected by the *National Sample Survey* (NSS), it is revealed for the 15-year period (1972-73 to 1981-88), that employment is estimated to have grown at the rate of 2.21 per cent per annum, rural employment has grown at the rate of 1.75 per cent per annum while urban employment has grown at a relatively much faster growth rate, around 4 per cent per annum. However, male and female employment has grown more or less at the same pace of around 2.2 per cent per annum and thus their relative shares in the total employment has remained more or less stationary at a ratio of 2:1 over the period. A study of trend in the growth rates of employment between organised and unorganised sectors reveals the both the sectors experienced a declining growth in employment.

During the last few decades women have entered the labour market in large numbers. This is as it should be. Women ought to be provided free space to take equal part in development fully. This is also a free condition for the advancement of the country. The role of women today is much broader – not the traditional role of wife and mother. Various careers are now open to women. Along with men they can go into a career life. Charles Handy, a management expert, has truly stressed upon, need of women's power in the organisations, "For these jobs the companies want quality people, well-educated, well skilled and adaptable. They also want people who can juggle with several tasks at one time, who are more interested in making things happen than in what title they hold or those who are more concerned with power and influence." He emphatically adds, "Organisations need talented women in their core jobs, therefore, not only for reasons of social fairness, important though that is, but because many of these women will have the kinds of attitudes and attributes that the new flexible organisations need. If they screen out the women they will handicap their futures." With education, women's role has changed. Instead of just being a housewife and mother, she can now become a companion to her husband and even a bread winner in the family. Today, the role of men and women overlap. The main reason and areas of those reasons are good facilities for higher education, Western influence, new economic opportunities and freedom given to women, new legal status arising out of social legislation, etc.[9]

However, there is still wide gender segregation in education, work participation, employment and occupational pattern all over the world. Women are in a disadvantageous position in social milieu and they are often prevented from carrying out a job successfully. They are treated unfairly when assigning individuals to supervisory position or managerial position in spite of similar career related attributes. A large number of respondents were found dissatisfied with their job as it underrated their education, remuneration was very low, chances of promotion were remote, had unhealthy working conditions, and suffered from lack of benefits. Sex segregation implies limited access to internal labour market and to their benefits for women. Women earn less than men in spite of similar qualifications and position.

Despite a slow and declining rate of employment growth the aggregate employment of the educated has been relatively high particularly among women. Educated employment growth rate was 7.5 per cent per annum for the last decade (1977-78 to 1987-88). According to an estimate nearly three-fourth of the unemployed belong to household with an income level less than Rs. 200 per month. All such families can be broadly classified as living below the poverty line.

By late 1970's it was realised that growth alone cannot solve these problems and that special programmes need to be introduced. "The Sixth Plan with its exclusive emphasis on the Integrated Rural Development had taken a step in the right direction. It made a fundamental departure from the approach towards development in the past plans. It was for the first time in the history of planning in India that employment was being considered more important than growth."[10] The Eighth Five Year Plan aimed at reducing unemployment to a negligible level within a reasonable period. A number of special employment programme for self and wage employment were being implemented in rural and urban areas. Solving the problem of growing unemployment in the urban areas a scheme called self-employment for educated unemployed was launched in 1983-84. The scheme aimed at encouraging the educated youth to undertake self-employment in industry, business and service sector. Yet another scheme, called self-employment programmes for the urban poor was started by the government in 1986. As the problem of educated unemployed youths had been aggravating for the last few years, the government focused special attention on the solution of the problem. The declaration of Prime Minister's Rozgar Yojna for educated unemployed youth was a step in this direction. "Educated unemployed, such as matriculate or matric failed do not get work because, perhaps their qualification is too insufficient or even otherwise there is no ready employment. These youths are provided training, loan and other facilities to run their own enterprise under PMRY."[11]

During 1993-94, two new programmes were launched which were (i) Employment Assurance Scheme (EAS) and (ii) Prime Minister's Rozgar Yojana (PMRY) for educated unemployed youth. The EAS was being implemented in 1,778 backward blocks in which a Revamped Public Distribution system was in operation. It aimed at providing 100 days of unskilled manual work to rural poor seeking employment. The PMRY scheme for educated unemployed youth was designed to provide employment to more than one million persons by setting up seven lakh micro enterprises during the Eighth Plan period in industry, service and business. The scheme for self-employment for educated unemployed youth was integrated with PMRY.

Another scheme, viz., Prime Minister's Urban Poverty Eradication Programme (PMUVPEP) was launched d1995-96, which apart from other things, aimed at employment generation and skill upgradation. The Integrated Rural Development Programme (IRDP, 6th plan) promoted self-employment by providing productive asset and inputs to the rural poor through a mix of subsidy and bank credit. Training Rural Youth for Self-Employment (TRYSEM) and Development of Women and Children in Rural Areas (DWCRA, 1982-87) were two special schemes of the IRDP. TRYSEM provides training and skill development opportunities to poor rural youth to enable them to take up self-employment or wage employment; DWACRA seeks to promote economic activities among the poorest of the poor rural women. The Jawahar Rojgal Yojana (JRY), started during 1986-89 was designed to generate additional short-term gainful employment for the rural unemployed and underemployed on works which create productive economic assert in rural areas. The Nehru Rojgar Yojana (NRY) was launched in October 1989 for the benefit of the urban poor.

Poverty

Among the economic reasons which have come in the way of women's education, poverty of parents is the chief cause. Parents cannot afford to spend on their children's education.[12] Indian economy is in a badshape after a decade of the reforms. Fundamental problems such as poverty, unemployment, lower productivity and ever increasing inequality are still alarming. The rising magnitude of unemployment led to a high incidence of poverty. A prevalent fact of unemployment in India is that the problem is more widespread in the families which are living below the poverty line, as due to lack of financial resources they cannot compete with moneyed people in acquisition of higher education, better training and higher social status of rich families.

Poverty is a socio-economic phenomenon which defies any process of definition; its concepts and content varies from country to country depending upon what a particular society accepts a reasonably good living standard for its people. Thus, in California, U.S.A., it would not be surprising if a family owning less than two cars may be dubbed as poor. People below the poverty line comprise largely those whose consumption is very low and who have little physical resources of production. In India, poverty manifests itself in its starkest form as a visual of semi-starved, ill clad, deprived millions of countrymen, thousands of them dying every day from malnutrition, ill-health and lack of basic amenities, a picture which is both appalling and agonising from any standard of human existence. Reduction of poverty ratio by 5 percentage points by 15 percentage points by 2012; providing gainful high-quality employment to the addition to the labour force over the Tenth Plan period.[13]

There is lack of regular and systematic survey about the extent of poverty. Rising living standards and poverty reduction across the globe are to a great extent the result of education and technological advances. The economic pressure to which man and his family is subjected to necessarily causes appreciable increase in the volume of illiteracy.

Traditional Complacency

The traditional complacency has always pulled back the women towards the kitchen. In a family, the girls or women had no right to property.[14] It is to be noted that not only the males, the women themselves, too, are a stumbling block for the women to grow and develop. The significant upshot of the reservation for women is the active role of the panchayat in solving cases of domestic violence, mostly dowry-related cases or others related to alcoholism. The problems of women arise from the lack of harmony between their developed individuality and aspirations on one hand and a conservative and backward state of society on the other.[15] It is need of the hour, that women should put their foot forward to build a strong educated society. It is true that today a good number of girls who go in for high school education stop there as they mostly get married and, therefore, settle down to their domestic duties.[16] It is the duty of every educated woman to motivate other women around them to be educated. The women should struggle against any injustice faced by them.

Child Labour

Successful introduction of free and compulsory education up to the age of 14 will no doubt accelerate the pace of women's education and will be helpful in eliminating child labour. The problem to educate girls in the age group 11-4 years in rural areas in relation to the aspiration and attitudes of the girls and their parents towards education. Girls in rural areas from lower economic strata of the society do not attend schools and the educational level of such families whose girls do not attend schools is very low. Girls from such families either help their parents in work or earn their own livelihood. When asked about child labour and bonded labour, each and every respondent was of the opinion that generally girls leave school at an early age and they work either at home or in farms. The category of bonded labourers who are not only engaged in agriculture but in large number of manufactories, mines and quarries can also be added too. However, when they fall in the wrong hands, the results can be disastrous that affect the judgement and behaviour of a person and can put a person at risk of unwanted activity and crime. In the landmark judgment the Supreme Court of India in July 1992 declared education as a fundamental right and the state was under a constitutional mandate to provide educational institutions at all levels for the benefit of citizens. Later the Supreme Court modified its judgment (1993) so as to confine the scope to elementary education, that the citizens of the country have a fundamental right to education. Even child / citizen of this country has a right to free education until he completes the age of 14 years. On the other hand, Article 45 of the Constitution of India states that the state shall endeavour to provide, within a period of ten years from the commencement of this Constitution, free and compulsory education for all children until they complete the age of 14 years. The mentioned judgments of the Supreme Court assume utmost significance.

The judgment of the Supreme Court had started a process in constituting the Muki Ram Saikia Committee (1997), to consider the implication of making elementary education a fundamental rights. However, the committee did not suggest central legislation making elementary education compulsory. But it suggested the government should be required to provided accessible schooling facilities to all and parents should treat it as their fundamental duty to send their children to school. There are those who feel that the existing provisions of the Constitution, for example, Articles 39, 41, 45, and 46, take care of what is intended in the Amendment.

But the amendment is needed for a variety of reasons. Firstly, it will induce the state and the people to make a special effort towards reaching this goal. Secondly, compulsory school education has been part and parcel of the civilised world. In as many as 161 countries, there are some degree of compulsion in school education. Only 23 countries have no legislation making education compulsory among which nine are in Africa and nine in Asia. Thirdly, the existing provisions are vague and ambiguous regarding the concept of education. Article 25 refers to education and non-formal schooling although, non-formal, informal, literacy campaign and any sort of education is equivalent to formal education. Fourthly, the existing legislation only indicates that the state government has the power to make education compulsory. Fifth, it is also the experience that voluntarism did not work during the last fifth years either on the part of the government or on the part of the people.

Compulsion is difficult to enforce but there is no choice for independent India. A proper mechanism has to be developed for enforcing compulsion. It is also argued that there is no ethical justification to compel the parents to send their children to poor quality school. Similarly, compulsion could cause hardship to the poor in the short run as children are withdrawn from the labour market. In the interim, the government has to develop a package of financial and other incentive for the poor; after all, as the abolition of child labour is also an explicitly stated goal of the government, so a financial package would serve a twin purpose. Thus, elementary education makes for a human resource development, which involves a better absorption of new information, new processes of production and through all that a better contribution to productivity and growth. It has been observed that a decline in illiteracy tends to reduce the fertility and infant mortality rates. One step to ease the problem is to send children to schools. Controlling population should be the top priority.

Child Marriage

The girls were considered as a burden on their parents until they were married. When we look into the past we see that child marriage and marriage at an early age prevailed in rural society and as well as in the civilised urban society. Customs of child marriage was deeply rooted in the society, therefore the question of their education was hardly thought of.[17]

This is implied that takeover of family responsibility was the main factor behind this thinking, and education was not considered to be important. The pernicious custom child marriage is responsible for many evils in the country. It is time that people realise of this fact that women education cannot advance unless there is social reconstruction through compulsory education and the prevention of child marriage. Therefore, compulsory education to the girl is to make her a useful member of society and create in her a desire for more knowledge. Therefore the basic education should be made compulsory for girls as much as possible. All the respondents were of the opinion that barring some cases of child marriage, due to education and psychcological change in the society the age of marriage of girls is steadily rising.

Discrimination against Women by Birth (Bhrunn Hatya)

If a female is murdered before her birth, how we can say that there is empowerment to women in India? This type of discrimination should be strictly punished by the implementation authority of laws. The psychology of human being needs to be changed by whole society, especially educated women, intellectual and by the respective state governments.

When a girl-child is born, the gender bias is evident and this needs to be eliminated. The girl needs to be treated on par with her brothers. The girl should get the feeling that she is an integral part of the family and not a burden. It is unimaginable that any civilised society will actually kill the baby girls at birth. This is the mother, who first started discriminating between boys and girls at home and in the outside world. Most of the time it is observed that the mother of the girl-child feels depressed for not having delivered a male child. She must change and the occasion for rejoicing should be for having brought a healthy child into this world. The father of a child also has an important role to play for accepting the girl-child at equal status to the male child. Furthermore, the society also needs to break the shackles of sympathising with the parents of the girl-child. Society will have to raise itself above this distinction of boy and girl and treat all children as the creation of God having equal right to live honourably in the world.

There is a preoccupation with the sexual and reproductive behaviour of females. Allowing for variations of behaviour across regions and between higher and lower castes, it is generally true that in India a woman's sense of personal worth is related to her fertility performance and the social standing she achieves as a mother of sons.[18] In rural areas women are treated very badly by their family members if they give birth to a female baby.[19]

Values are the keys to the survival of human beings. They are love, trust, joy, dignity, acceptance, truth, compromise, and respect for the individual understanding and reverence. The reactions became somehow dramatic and tense when we asked respondents about their feelings on the same issue. Concern over the continuing decline in the sex ratio and rising incidence of female foeticide, stressed the needs for an immediate action plan to maintain social equilibrium, stressing the need for every citizen in the country to be part of this process. This is fundamental right and you can't put clogs in the way of a citizen exercising his right.

Male-dominated Society (Purush Pradhan Samaj)

The society as a whole is male-dominated and patriarchal in nature. Male domination has had some very unfortunate effects. It has made the most initiative human relations, that of marriage, one of master and slave, instead of one between equal partners. Women have been dominated by males and the traditions evolved by the male-dominated society. The family system was paternal and the eldest male member was the final authority. This aspect subjugated the role of woman in social life. A girl played no important role in the family. The role of women was limited and restricted to home life, especially looking after children, elders and their husbands.[20]

The inclination on the part of the women for participation in public affairs and self-determination has been largely stymied. In some areas, women members are not given due respect by their male counterparts, sometimes, the male steer the women members by remote control, using their dominance in the family mainly. The traditional culture system which has struck its roots deep in the system, is responsible for this unfortunate development. Still the society as a whole is male-dominated and patriarchal in nature. Undoubtably by bringing more and more women in day-to-day activities of three-tier panchayat system, the government has emboldened them a lot. Even then, the women are not completely shackle-free.

In this male-dominated society which the woman has so generously allowed, the idea of providing empowerment to women seems quite ironic. The woman has complete control over her child before birth, allows him to rule over her, proves her generosity. Indian women, thus, can be described as the underdogs of society where, though in theory, the law of equality is practised and women are considered to be on par with their male counterparts, in reality, the men remain powerful and thrive at the expense of the women.[21]

It appears that with the empowerment of women the attitude towards them should be changed. Empowerment has provided them to find ways to grow and develop more, almost equally with her male counterpart. But without a change in attitude in males, the development will be stalled. In the progressive society of tomorrow, life should be a joint venture for men and women. So either in a family or in an office males must consider the women members as capable as they are. For this attitudinal change the society as a whole needs to be more liberal, more frank, setting aside the age-old attitude towards women. Women have always suffered in a male-dominated society and have to fight their basic rights in all societies. They are still fighting, more so in the Third World countries including India.

Curricula and teaching materials remain gender-biased to a large degree, and are rarely sensitive to the specific needs of girls and women. This reinforces traditional female and male roles that deny women opportunities for full and equal partnership in society. Lack of gender awareness by educators at all levels strengthens existing inequities between males and females by reinforcing discriminatory tendencies and undermining the girls' self-esteem. The lack of sexual and reproductive health education has a profound impact on women and men.

Women are often considered subsidiary and complementary to men which is considered as crucial and dominating. Women's rights regarding training, employment and carrer advancement have received only secondary importance. However, women all over the world are discriminated only on the basis of being a female. Almost all countries of the world are guilty of treating women as inferior to men.

Justice to all and appeasement of none would be the guiding principle for social harmony. Insecurity breeds suspicion and, together, these undermine the norms of an open society. Any act is then under threat. There is denial of natural justice merely because the entire process of decisionmaking is being completed by men. It has to be left to the collective wisdom of the people including women to decide, and should not involve the decision of an individual but the collective will which in turn will reflect the will of the people. If we do not meet the challenge to continue to give a competition others will emerge that will replace us. It would be unforgivable to refuse to improve women's capacity in the process of reclaiming hope, humanity, equality and dignity—birthrights that were stripped by society at large. If women don't realise this, they will fail to harness their inherited powers. Coming out of the ignorance about self will rid them of the problem of the day and bring them fully into the present. This collective will is entitled to send a message to our leaders.

Eve-Teasing and Sexual Harassment

There is no woman who has not suffered at one time or another harassment, humiliation, exploitation and violence that shadows her sex. A woman's life lies between pleasure at one end and danger at other. In daily life women are routinely defined by sex, and even if not all men are potential kidnappers, rapists, batterers and murderers of women, all women are potential victims.

Sexual harassment at workplace violates a person's sense of dignity and the right to earn a living with dignity. It is against the fundamental rights embodied in the Indian Constitution and also against basic human rights. A mechanism has to be set up for addressing that problem and give it more focus and emphasis.

Undoubtedly, harassment and violence against the helpless has been the most shameful and horrendous evil in our society. Issues from female genital mutilation, rape, child abuse, lesbian sex are thought important and now have become a high-profile movement that highlights violence against women. Women's attitudes towards their own rising and raising empowering feminist feelings in an uneducated middle class have to do with the majority of educated women in this country.

Purdah Pratha

Gandhiji was opposed to the Purdah system and considered it as slavery for women. In the Midle East countries, women are not even allowed to show their faces or go to the market. It is certain that these women never think of working, not even in the wildest of their dreams. Women kept within four walls of house cannot breathe freely. Purdah does not develop character, it develops from within. People by and large live a miserable life and in a country, the pernicious custom of purdah is responsible for many evils in the country. The evil of purdah must go through appreciable advancement in education of women. A strong public opinion must be created to fight against this evil which hamper our national progress. Compromise of principles and ethical standards at all level is widespread and known to all sections of people. We all have to adopt new approaches to face the challenge squarely. There should be strict rules to keep them in check; these are achievable objectives.

Sati Pratha

Beliefs fuel actions and our belief system governs our everyday decisions and actions that we take in life. Humans are the only species in the world that can interpret and apply meaning to things beyond the literal physical level of reality. These interpretations and meanings help us to make decisions and act accordingly. Sikh Gurus were the first to be against the evil of 'Sati'. Guru Amar Das said, "Blessed are those who lead a life of containment and chastity." Even after 60 years of independence, and much advancement in science and technology and drastic social change the genuine place of women could not be ascertained by attracting them towards education and providing them a respectable and suitable place in the society.

Dowry and Dowry Death

The Joint Committee of Parliament appointed in December 1981 to examine the Dowry Prohibition Act 1961 with a view to suggesting amendment to effectively deal with this social menace took evidence all over the country and submitted a report in 1982. The Bill to amend the provisions of the Act was passed by Parliament in 1984. Before taking evidence, the Joint Committee had circulated a questionnaire asking comments and proposals for improvements in the Act.[22] The Dowry Prohibition Act 1961 bans the practice of dowry, but in reality all that the law does is to recognise that the problem exists. It is virtually unheard of for a husband or his family to be sued for insisting on taking a dowry. If anything, the demands for dowry have escalated over the years along with dowry deaths. At a modest estimate, the figure for deaths in India that occur due to non-payment or partial payment of dowry could be placed around 4, 000 for one year. Delhi police recorded 421 cases of bride-burning in 1980, 568 in 1981, 619 in 1982, and 371 between 1 January 1983 and 30 November, 1983.[23]

Dowry does not have any place in Sikhism. According to Sikh ideology there is only one kind of dowry, i.e., of "Hari Naam" that a woman should possess and bring with her. Gurbani accords equal status to both men and the women, laying emphasis on the development of their respective qualities without any attempt to subjugate the other. Both men and women, with their respective attributes and roles are to bring fulfilness in the family life. The greatest obstacle towards social change is conservativeness of woman herself. She thinks a woman is unfortunate and supports the dowry system to increase wealth. She cannot see another woman working outside home and spreads rumours, like working women are bad mothers and inefficient housewives.

Alcoholism

Gandhiji was a moralist, so he was against wine and drugs; taking wine was worse than thieving and prostitution. To him drinking is a disease which causes a lot of harm to human body. Drinking ruins the nation. For long, women were the most repressed section even in their families. In present times there are various kinds of conflicts happening within and around us. There are few employment opportunities as a result of which there is a lot of resentment and frustration among the youth and the illiterate poor men booze and beat their wives during the night. Women are unable to protest against the daily hazard. The adverse impact of this evil can therefore be attributed primarily to the failures of the social system. The voice of women should be heard and be treated as a human right issue by communities. Economic and educational developments are the two main components in the process of eradication of this evil. Cent per cent respondents were of the opinion that government and welfare agencies should get a first-hand knowledge of the problems being faced by the women, make an indepth study of the same and deliver services including education and health, which would help in the eradication of illiteracy in the womenfolk and to become part and parcel of the process of development.

Gender Discrimination in Health Sector

Health is not just a medical or economic issue, but a vital dimension of social justice. The political agenda must embrace the removal of discrimination against the girl-child and give place to the empowerment of women and full legal equality. It must also ensure dignity to the most vulnerable and deprived sections of society, such as the women and children affected. The lives of millions of women and children hang in balance today as each year pregnancy and childbirth claim the lives of half a million women and more than 10 million children; this tragedy had to end. The Tenth Five Year Plan calls for "Reduction in the decadal rate of population growth between 2001 and 2011 to 16.2 per cent; Increase in literacy rate to 75 per cent within the Plan period; Reduction of infant mortality rate (MR) to 45 per 1,000 live births by 2007 and to 28 by 2012; Reduction of maternal mortality ratio (MMR) to 2 per 1,000 live births by 2007 and to 1 by 2012."[24]

Majority of respondents called for highest national and international political commitment to maternal, newborn and child health and requests government to commit the required resources and appeal integrated approach to reproductive maternal, newborn and child health ensuring a continuum of care from pregnancy through childhood. Government must design and implement programmes that are tailored to the needs and realities of national and regional settings were their suggestions. Non-governmental organisation are needed for upliftment of deprived sections of society all over the country and also urged upon the government to come to the aid of such initiatives.

Rape and Trafficking of Women

The weaker section of society, women, are unable to understand or appreciate the cumbersome procedural wrangles and suffering from hesitancy and lack of cohesion. Indian women lack in power and endurance. We should work on these aspects and stress on improvment in these areas. Crimes against women will decline only if the mindset of men towards women change. Until then the goal of empowerment of women will remain a distant dream. The crime rate, even in the United States of America against women, makes one shudder. For instance, a woman is raped in the United States every 40 seconds as per the findings of the National Victim Centre / Crime Victims Research and Treatment Centre, 1992. The position of women in underdeveloped and developing countries is even worse. Virginity is valued by men, yet it is men who violate it and commit rapes. The important factors in rape are "age", "consent" (including implied consent and obtaining consent under fraudvelent protext of marriage), "duress", "state of mind" and "resistance". Section 375 of the Indian Penal Code describes rape as sex with a women against her will, or without her consent, or with her consent obtained by putting her in fear or death or hurt, or with her consent when the man knows that he is not her husband but she believes him as her husband, or with or without her consent when she is under 16 years of age. The rape problem is considered serious in many countries. In the United States the annual rate of rape offences is about 26, in Canada B. O. and in U. K. 5.4 per one lakh of total population. The number of registered rape cases in 1974 was 53,400 in U.S.A., 2,843 in Canada and 1,494 in U.K.[25]

Incidents of child rape had increased in 1998 by 8 per cent, while incidents of abetment to suicide and procuration of minor girls had gone up by 115.4 and 96.6 per cent, respectively. The incidence of selling girls for prostitution increased by 22.2 per cent while child rate victims (below 16 years) alone accounted for 27 per cent.[26]

A majority of the people in the Third World are under the line of poverty and the countries in the Asian region like Bangladesh, India, Nepal, Pakistan and Sri Lanka are no exception to it. The people have been deprived of adequate access in the basic needs of life such as health, education, housing, food, security, employment, gender justice and development and a large number of them starve to death every year, which has resulted in increasing human misery causing trafficking of women and children. Trafficking of women and children is one of the worst violations of human rights. It is a matter of great concern that even after half a century since the adoption of the Universal Declaration of Human Rights by the international community, trafficking continues to be rising at a great pace. The International Organisation for Migration (IOM) estimates that global trafficking industry generates up to eight billions of U.S. dollars each year from what may be described as 'trade in human misery'.

Human trafficking is a very difficult concept to understand due to the variety of forms it takes. There are many forms of trafficking. But the most visible and widespread is the trafficking of women and children for commercial exploitation. This kind of exploitation of women and children is not a new phenomenon. Its origin goes to the history and tradition of many countries. It is very difficult to detect the number of people who are involved in this business at an early stage. This is because people who are being trafficked have an illusion that traffickers are supporting them and their family by arranging work for them at other places. Today, South Asia has emerged alongside South-East Asia as a major centre of intra- and international trafficking of women and children. Trafficking of women is done primarily for the purpose of prostitution, and forced marriages. Though there is dearth of hard accurate data, the fact remains that this volume of trafficking of women and children in India is disproportionately high. The pace at which trafficking is being conducted presents a great challenge for those who are making laws to fight with this problem. However, this problem has now been expanded by globalisation and its linkage with lucrative tourist and sex industries. Though it is a global phenomenon, the problem has assumed alarming dimensions in different countries of Asia, and particularly South Asia.

The laws vary considerably from country to country, and in most of the cases they are directly linked to trafficking of women and girls for the purposes of prostitution. In this regard the definition adopted in the SAARC Convention is much narrower to be a universally accepted definition. According to SAARC "Trafficking in persons" shall mean the recruitment, transportation, transfer, harbouring or receipt of persons, by means of the threat or use of force or other forms of coercion, of abduction, of fraud, of deception, of the abuse of power or of a position of vulnerability or of the giving or receiving of payments or benefits to achieve the consent of a person having control over another person, for the purpose of exploitation. Exploitation shall include, at a minimum, the exploitation of the prostitution of others or other forms of sexual exploitation, forced labour or services, slavery or practices similar to slavery, servitude or the removal of organs. There is no consensus on single definition of trafficking. This is termed as movement of persons through force, or violence for exploitative purpose. Some intellectuals also term migration through illegal means as trafficking but all kinds of illegal migration are not trafficking and the basic distinction between the two is the question of consent. The definition adopted by UN states that a person may be trafficked into a variety of harmful circumstances, including forced prostitution, bonded labour, or slavery-like working conditions. Anti-trafficking laws of some of the South Asian countries focus primarily on prostitution, and do not require a separate showing of coercion, deception or other abuses, women and girls engaged in commercial sex work may be presumed to have been trafficked and all trafficked women being tagged as prostitutes. Women and girls trafficked into prostitution are treated as criminals under national anti-prostitution laws of the some countries, and the human rights of these cannot be protected as committed by the international agencies.

Traffickers manipulate people's poor economic condition to their advantage. Families from poor communities in rural areas, who are in dire economic straits, become easy victims of the traffickers who offer them either job or proposal for marriage. Neglect of human rights also invite trafficking. Factors which are responsible and helping traffickers are inadequate employment opportunities for women, lack of social safety, globalisation, discriminatory laws and social practices that restrict women's and girls' access to education and economic security, forced or coerced marriages. Difficult economic conditions, oppression and torture of the girls and prevailing social discrimination against girl-child and woman in Bangladesh and Nepal today are some of the causative factors and are the largest source of child prostitutes to Indian brothels. A UNICEF survey indicates that from 5,000 to 7,000 girls are trafficked to India every year. Trafficked women and children are used for varieties of purposes like prostitution, domestic work, illegal adoption of children, organ transplant, begging, drug- trafficking, forced marriages and various other exploitative form of work.

The status of women has always been of great concern in the past. Women in India and other countries have struggled to establish an identity and create a space in social sphere. There is a need for advancement towards the goals of equality, development and empowerment for all women in the interest of all the communities and humanity. Women need means of finding their way through the day-to-day reality of living in the way that supports their desires. This major effort is expected to give us a solid experience for our future development. Our old patterns of thinking and doing don't give us the guidance we need to actualise our ideals and transform our lives. Women should look at themselves, moving closer to the truth of who they are. As we face challenges and move through difficulties, many times we feel lonely, isolated or misunderstood by others. In doing so, they will move beyond the limitations of their bonded personalities and the world around them will begin to transform. They all know their past lives, their dreams, frustration, relationship, their different personalities, they have learned lessons that are being taught by the discriminated society, all possible choices, the past and their potential future. Their choices will take them towards their highest good! A clear shift is visible from the "me-myself" to a broader society. For women education and career is a natural process of growing up. They search for newer opportunities and face challenges with ease and seek fulfilment in career. We have to relocate the efforts and laws pertaining to women's concerns and bring together those pieces that are scattered around the world to provide a sustainable organised to promote efforts in a shared manner. Geographical boundaries have become irrelevant in today's open economies and globalisation era.

Ever since the launching of SAARC in 1985 as an association of states with aims to promote the well-being of the populations of South Asia and improve their standard of living; to speed up economic growth, social progress and cultural development; to reinforce links between the countries of this area; and, lastly, to promote mutual collaboration and assistance in the economic, social, cultural technical and scientific fields, issues related to women have figured prominently on the SAARC agenda. In 1986 the Technical Committee on Women in Development was created under the Integrated Programme of Action (IPA). Formulation of the Regional Plan of Action on Women was the result after 13 meetings of the Technical Committee being held under IPA. In January 2000 it was then merged into the Technical Committee on Social Development under the SAARC Integrated Programme of Action (SIPA). This Committee on Social Development didn't last long and ceased to work with the creation of a new Technical Committee on Women, Youth and Children under the revised Regional Integrated Programme of Action (RIPA) in January 2004.

Concerned over the trafficking of women and children within and between countries in the region, SAARC adopted a Regional Convention on Combating the Crime of Trafficking in Women and Children for Prostitution in January 2002, during the Eleventh Summit in Kathmandu. The Convention asked member parties for cooperation in dealing with various aspects of prevention, interdiction and suppression of trafficking in women and children for prostitution, and repatriation and rehabilitation of victims of trafficking. It asked the parties for prevention of use of women and children in international prostitution networks, from the countries where it originates, transited and destined. The Thirteenth Summit (Dhaka, 12-13 November 2005) affirmed strongly to resolve to work together to combat the problem created by trafficking in women and children.

SAARC called for cooperation from other international communities and in the process signed a Memorandum of Understanding (MoU) with the United Nations Development Fund for Women (UNIFEM), to help member countries to march towards empowerment to achieve the goals of gender equality. The MoU was signed in December 2001. Under the MoU, SAARC and UNIFEM are in the process of developing the SAARC Gender Database: Mapping Progress of Women in the South Asia Region.

Simultaneously political level consultations are bieng held towards the cause of women. Many ministerial conferences have been convened to address the specific concerns of women at Shillong (1986), Islamabad (1990), Kathmandu (1993), and Dhaka (1995) and Pakistan (2006). The Ministerial Conference in Dhaka adopted a "Dhaka Resolution on Women", which was later presented to the Fourth World Conference on Women (Beijing, 1995).

At the highest political level, the leaders have continued to stress on the need to address issues affecting women. At their Eleventh Summit (Kathmandu, January 2002), the leaders agreed to mobilise necessary resources and to intensify broad-based action to achieve a set of priority goals in improving the social status of women and children. These include, among others (a) establishing a voluntary fund with the contribution from Member States, individuals, donor countries and agencies for rehabilitation and reintegration of the victims of trafficking; and (b) pursuing and promoting social development through empowerment of women and ensuring their full participation in decision making at all levels. At that Summit, the leaders also reaffirmed their commitment to the upliftment of social status of women in the region through specific and target-oriented programmes. They also directed that necessary measures be taken to ensure the development of women to their inherent potential.

Pursuant to a decision of the Eleventh Summit (Kathmandu, January 2002), the SAARC Autonomous Women's Advocacy Group (SAWAG) was formed, to advocate mainstreaming gender and make recommendation on gender-related issues and programmes in the region. The Group convened its first meeting in June 2004 in Islamabad, and decided to commission a study incorporating issues such as women's citizenship, women's political representation, trafficking and sexual exploitation, gender and HIV/AIDS, female education and literacy, legal rights and economic empowerment and impact of globalisation on women.

The Thirteenth Summit (Dhaka, 12-13 November 2005) reiterated its pledge to continue to work in the next decade and beyond to address the formidable challenges faced by women and children, especially the girl-child. That Summit noted that sustained efforts were needed on the part of the Member States not only to free them from all types of deprivation but also to make them full partners and beneficiaries of South Asian progress and development.

Trafficking in human beings has become a subject of great concern to many South Asian countries. Several legal and policy initiatives are being undertaken by many nations in this region, in order to address this phenomenon. In September 2004, governments from the South Asia region met in Colombo, Sri Lanka, at mid-term to review of the implementation of their commitments towards human trafficking. The Indian Constitution is very clear on this subject. Article 23 of Part III of the Constitution related to fundamental rights under the caption "Right Against Exploitation" prohibits trafficking of the human beings and provides that any contravention of this right shall be an offence punishable by law. The Directive Principles of State Policy under Part IV of the Constitution in Article 39 (e) and (k) declare that state policies should be directed towards securing that the "childhood and youth are protected against exploitation and material abandonment."

India was concerned over this problem much before the international communities had taken this issue as a concern. Taking the constitutional principles as the base the Suppression of Immoral Traffic in Women and Girls Act was enacted in 1956. The Act was amended in 1986 and ratified as the Immoral Traffic (Prevention) Act. The amended Act continues to prohibit prostitution in its commercialised form without making prostitution *per se* an offence. The Act prescribes stringent action against those procuring children for the purpose of prostitution. If the offence is committed against a child, the punishment is rigorous imprisonment for a term not less than seven years. Regrettably, enforcement of the Act by the state governments has been extremely poor. Cases of clandestine inter-state and cross-border trafficking in women and girls are seldom thoroughly investigated. Consequently, the basic structure of the cruel and exploitative system remains intact and continues to flourish.

Section 13 (4) of the Act empowers the central government to appoint trafficking police officers with nationwide jurisdiction for the investigation of cases of inter-state trafficking in women. No step has so far been taken by the government in this regard to appoint 'Trafficking Police Officers'. A central investigation agency, notably the Central Bureau of Investigation, should be directed by the government to perform the functions of Section

13 of the Act which clearly states that the state governments should appoint special police officers who should be assisted by an advisory body comprising leading social welfare workers of the era. This, if done, will create a mechanism at the field level to initiate and sustain appropriate action. Indeed, effective implementation of the provisions of the IPTA needs far greater police vigilance. It is the police connivance which often enables the pimps and traffickers to operate without fear and get away scot-free. Moreover, cross-border trade in women and children is not possible without the involvement and support of the police and the personnel of the Border Security Force.

Increased political and social consciousness in the region on the issues of elimination of gender-disparity and empowerment of women which are essential for their socio-economic development has made the leaders of national governments to address these issues through further affirmative action. The leaders noted the progress in the implementation of the Plan of Action to mark 1991-2000 as the 'SAARC Decade of the Girl-Child', and requested the council of ministers to conduct a comprehensive mid-decade review for presentation to the Ninth SAARC Summit. Considering that the exploitation of the girl-child is a direct reflection of the status of women in society, the leaders reaffirmed their resolve to take necessary measures to eliminate all forms of discrimination against women and girl-children. The progress in this has been uneven, inequalities between women and men have persisted and major obstacles remain, with serious consequences for the well-being of all people. Much of the work of SAARC has occurred at a level, where leaders are involved in providing important services to vulnerable communities especially women in areas as diverse as health care, education and professional training, legal advice, humanitarian relief and women's empowerment.

Leaders have realised the urgency of the situation and are creating an atmosphere conducive to good performance. This will give all the energy to women, leaders and all those who believe in the good and for this we all have to take care of the empowerment of women and their development in their social status.

Concluding Observation

Most of the Indian women have been suffering from the lack of self and space, disempowerment, disprivilege, disadvantage, sexist, discrimination, gender inequality, invisibility, asymmetries, marginalisation, revalorisation and reification.[27] These are open questions today, and require a great deal of intellectual debate. In India, women are way ahead of women elsewhere in the matter of social legislation. But the implementation of laws granting rights to women has been so slow, lopsided and haphazard that socially, economically and politically women are kept for behind the men.[28] The question is how to empower women so that she feels independent, confident and takes up any type of responsibility to perform. Respondents advised government to live up to its promise and decision to implement women's education and employment generation sectors and would be given priority. Thus, to raise the economic and social level of women government should plan policies, which can help and support the women, which will be an investment and a new infrastructure.

The state of mind, which is an outcome of past or future incidence or tasks, makes a person less cautious while at work. While women may have the potential to sustain in a high pressure environment, they may not have the patience to bear with the same environment for long. They will have to wait till the break is achieved and then think of some future course of action and take a positive attitude to all developments; it is the only chance we see for a sustainable future. Psychological dimensions, therefore, need to be considered with equal concern, while analysing the phenomenon of development. Formal and non-formal education, religious institution, mass media should act along this line. We must educate our youth to feel, think and act for a better world. The most simple method, author believes, to empower women is to start respecting her first at home and then everywhere else including her work place. Empowerment, believe it, will follow automatically.

References

1. Ewing, Gulshan Ewing, Indira Gandhi Talks about Women and International Women's Year, *Eve's Weekly*, 1975.

2. S. B. Rai, *Society and Education in India (1813-1857)*, 1955.
3. Uttam Kumar Singh, *Women Education*, Commonwealth Publishers, New Delhi, 1997, p. 218.
4. The Government of India, *The National Sample Survey Organisation*, Department of Statistics, Ministry of Planning, Vol. XIV, No.4, Issue No.47, April-June, 1991, p.26.
5. Approach Paper to the Tenth Five Year Plan (2002-2007), Planning Commission, The Government of India, New Delhi, September, 2001, p. 3.
6. L Misra, *Education of Women in India from 1921 to 1955*, 1961.
7. *Miracle of Teaching*, vol. VII, No. 1, Jan-April-2007, p.25.
8. K. M. Naidu, Unemployment and Employment in India: An Overview, *Indian Journal of Labour Economics*, January-March, 1993, p.8.
9. P. Ramachandran, *Women and Education*, Tata Institute of Social Science, 1963.
10. Trilok Singh, 'Employment and Planning – Assessment and Strategies in India', *Indian Economic Journal*, April-June 1986, pp.51-54.
11. Extract from the speech of Prime Minister P. V. Narasimha Rao on 15 August 1993.
12. Maithili Vishwanathan, *Development Orientation of Women's Education*, Printwell, Jaipur, 1994, p.63.
13. *Approach Paper to the Tenth Five Year Plan (2002-2007)*, op. cit.
14. J. K. Dave, *A Study of Evolution of Female Education in Gujarat*, 1971.
15. C. Naik, *Education of Women in the Province of Bombay (1918-1947)*, 1949.
16. Vishwanathan, op. cit., p. 68.
17. Dave, op. cit.
18. H. Papanek, *Changing Women in Changing Society*, University of Chicago Press, 1973.
19. Bhola Nath Gosh, *Rural Women Leadership*, Mohit Publications, New Delhi, 2002, p. 99.
20. Dave, op. cit.
21. H. C. Upadhyay, *Status of Women in India*, Anmol Publications Pvt. Ltd. New Delhi. 1997, p. 183.
22. Ibid., p. 175.
23. *The Hindustan Times*, 18 December, 1983.
24. *Approach Paper to the Tenth Five Year Plan (2002-2007)*, op. cit.

25. West Roy and Nicholas, *Understanding Sexual Attacks*, Heinemann Educational Books Ltd., 1978 .
26. Spurt in Crimes Against Women, Warns Report, *Times of India*, New Delhi, 24 Feb. 2000. p.1.
27. Jugal Kishore Misra, Empowerment of Women in India, *Indian Journal of Political Science*, Vol. LXVII, No. 4, Oct-Dec., 2006.
28. Ram Ahuja, Research Report on "Awareness of Rights Among Women", 1982.

8

Women's Education: Calling Roles for Principle and Practice

BRIEF

The preamble of our Constitution lays down the general principles on which we wish to build up our state. The Preamble says that the objective of the Constitution is "to secure to all its citizens, justice, social, economic and political: liberty of thought, expression, belief, faith and worship: equality of status and of opportunity; and to promote among them all fraternity assuming the dignity of the individual and the unity of the nation." If this is to be our objective, then our education, whether that of men or of women, will have to undergo a radical change.[1]

Indian women have far greater visibility and voice than what they had 50 years ago. They have entered into and created impacts in every sphere of public activity. On the one hand, women must continue to claim rights and spaces for themselves, to enter new arenas of decision making, to participate in setting the agenda as well as in discussing agendas set by others. Women's presence and participation is now recognised as an essential condition for development in some soft sectors like primary education, health, sanitation, etc. Men and women must work together to ensure rights and freedom for all citizens.

Who can get success? One who starts the work and finishes, gets success. This line can be attributed to the empowerment and the success of women and also depend on the powerful thoughts which give confidence, good memory, control of body and brain, power to keep positive thoughts, hard work capacity, decision-taking capacity, discipline, etc. These thoughts should be supported by her family. She should also get trained with regard to the above to get success in life. Without powerful thoughts all the things and resources available to her are useless. Gandhiji said, "Educating a man is educating an individual while educating a women is educating a family." Women should have the same opportunity as men to fulfil their ambitions. However much needs to be done and government and other players in empowerment of women should lay special emphasis on women's participation in the education sector, to remove gender disparity from the point of view of development.

Role of Governments

The atmosphere is changing. Education has made a great impact in empowering women and there is some attention being paid to it since last few years that is a welcome development. Access of girls and women to all levels of education, including the higher level, and all academic areas is one of the factors of their continued progress in professional activities. The confidence-building measures taken have begun to bear fruit but more needs to be done to convince women and society. Increasingly overburdened, women will able to sort through work challenges. These programmes sound little out there but have a positive impact. It is important to keep things going when times aren't so good.

Some suggestions have been made for development of women in the Tenth Five Year Plan:

- Provide gainful (quality) employment to the addition to the labour forces over the Tenth Five Year Plan year.
- Reduce gender gaps in literacy and wage rates by at least 50 per cent by 2007.
- Increase literacy rates to 75 per cent within the plan period.
- The Tenth Five Year Plan has to initiate necessary steps to guarantee equal access and participation of women in decision-making bodies including the legislation, executive, judicial, corporate, statutory bodies, etc.
- Introduce women-friendly personnel policies which will be an additional feature in the Tenth Five Year Plan to

encourage women to participate effectively in all administrative decision-making proceses.

— Organise women into Self-Help Groups (SHGs).

The Tenth Five Year Plan strategy aims at a specific threefold strategy for empowering women which includes social empowerment, economic empowerment and gender justice.

Although our Constitution provides various rights for the women but still they aspire to full membership in the human race and there is always scope for improvement. The social welfare bodies of central government and the state governments should firmly first focus on the issue of helping people. The government should frame and implement policies and diversification programmes with a view to generate more and more employment opportunities. These efforts should be taken with multiple objectives of improving the employment avenues and improving state and national economy on which hinges the very economic survival of the entire region and nation. This can only be possible by identifying shortcomings and taking remedial measures.

Leaders and government should welcome all constructive criticisms of programmes, and success can be achieved only if attention is paid to methods in enhancing quality and value. They should have adequate knowledge of the sphere of operations at different levels before implementing the scheme. It is advisable to involve as many employees as possible in the interaction process for smooth implementation of the scheme. The government should provide them information about technical and physical parameters of the programme, present or past. It would be prudent to maintain a healthy relationship with all the sections of government machinery and it would be further fortified while the weaknesses removed. We have no more time for talking, the respondents were of the opinion that one should speed up the processes and the government, may it be state or centre, should follow national policies with a wider perspective for setting the stage for the massive development of women.

Role of Societies

For a long time Indian society has been treating the womenfolk as the lowest among the lowest in social status. In our conditions, the role of education is to transform a static society into vibrant one with a commitment to development and change. An important element of this metamorphosis is the emergence of a learning society in which people of all ages and sections not only have access to education but also get involved in the process of continuing education.[2] Education is the key that opens the door in life which is essentially social in character.[3] In the author's views society is rarely concerned with women's role about social, economic or political matters. Many portrayed women in limited, stereotyped ways and most failed to present women's perspectives or points of view on subjects that affect them directly. If women have financial freedom and education, but don't have the recognition of their work and efforts, in their home and social environment, then they cannot get success easily. Social recognition means support of their family and social environment for the women's work and decision inside home and outside world. A majority of the respondents were of the opinion that if society does not give recognition to any person, whether man or woman, he/she has no success in the true sense.

Education increases the mental status of a person. Illiteracy is one of the reasons for women not getting equal status in the society. Infrastructure for education should be up to the mark that will provide education to women and this can bring changes and strengthen them. What was not succeeded by legislation can be made practicable by education and enlarge the vision of the public. The value education will help women in reaching to many worlds of human experience that lie outside their walled world. It will also produce an enormous enrichment and make experiences of outer world an exciting place to live in. But education is not an all-time solution to the problem of women if not embedded with the attitude of society toward women's education. Without attitudinal change like all programmes, it will enforce its inevitable limits on women if women do not take pains to change themselves. It seems that the major challenge for value education now is to try to prevent the negative attitude of society and simply to help install its power in women. It is only education that can exercise intelligence, imagination, curiosity, and self-criticism to the fullest possible, so that as we add its contributions to the field of knowledge, we really realise its powers. This is the process of finding valuable new pockets of knowledge to fuel innovation. The process involves knowing what to look for, where to look for it and how to tap into a promising source, a mutual desire in developing wider and closer cooperation and understanding in regional and national affairs. According to Lady Platt of the Equal Opportunities Commission, "If a girl is well qualified and prepared to do her homework, then the world is her oyster."[4] In a multi-cultural society of India where caste, creed and religious are divergent, women often have to bear the major brunt of the socio-economic friction and end up as losers in the struggle for power. The continuing cases of amniocentesis, child marriage, female dropouts from schools, eve teasing, rapes, marital violence, dowry deaths, etc., are a sad commentary for a country like ours, which is traditionally known for holding women in high esteem. The number of women opting for professional education and managerial position has increased over the years. However, much more needs to be done and support given to women to enable them to quality and perform in professional services and management, and to set up their own enterprises. Some of the suggestions towards this objective are being given by the respondents and author herself:

- The policy thrust should include knowledge-based areas such as support for quality education in professional and management areas for women.
- Implementation of policies needs to be more effective and target-oriented.
- Management development programmes which are area-specific will be useful need to be promoted among women.
- Training and awareness programmes, financial assistance may be provided for professional and women entrepreneurs. Career and leadership programmes are also needed.
- Education and training programmes for men and women in order to learn how to manage gender diversity in society more effectively.
- Promotion of women teachers association / associations for state levels will be useful.

The Indian women can fulfil the dream of Gandhiji's concept of Ramrajya by restoring the moral and ethical values, by eliminating the corruption with an objective for the upliftment in the matter of politic, society, economy, welfare and administration. This is the most natural and universally accepted role of women in society, which is mostly recognised by the world's Human Rights Declaration for the upliftment in the matter of politics, society and administration. A society in which women are taught anything but the management of a family, the care of men and the creation of the future generation is a society which is on the way out.

Role of Teachers

International assignments are increasingly seen as an integral part of career development for potential women. Professional courses and degrees must train women to enter into new professions and move away from the traditional roles and low-paying jobs. Skill development of women have to be multifarious to enable sustainability. The self-efficacy level of women can be improved by organising workshops and training programmes.

The major handicaps for progress of girls' education in our country were inadequate fund, dearth of trained teachers and attitude of the parents of middle and lower classes to girls' education. The teacher must inculcate and transmit values through various effective media. Teachers have a vital role in the development of community life. The teachers' role is to develop desirable values and attitudes. Good education, proper care and provision of opportunities for creative expression, inspire, stimulate and sharpen creative mind and the role of teacher is to make significant contribution that is required to help girls in nourishing and utilising their creative abilities to the utmost. Effective teaching means sensitisation in many areas for enlarging vision that is critical to achieve success, not merely pedagogic accomplishments. The teacher's function does not end with just merely teaching the children, covering the syllabus, using textbooks. He has a more fundamental task of helping the child to choose its environment and to get the proper stimulation for its development.[5] The teacher should achieve certain common goals which are needed for development. The curricula quality of teachers and administration in all stages need greater attention.

Most of the respondents emphasised the contribution of teachers and their guidance. All were of the opinion that teachers should not simply teach on the basis of what has been told to them nor do they merely imitate the ways of teaching they have listened to. They have to build up their students with professional knowledge, skills and value perspectives, so they have to be their own masters, experts and decision makers. They further elaborated that it is the responsibility of teachers to prepare women to face the dilemma arising out of the eternal conflict between the ends and the means, which would be possible only if they themselves ideologically and pragmatically espouse the cause of ethical standards and values as being essential to long-term success. Illiteracy alone is not the problem, there is clear indication that the norms of behaviour exhibited by teachers are transmitted into future women, which increasingly influences the state of ethics in the society. Good education will make us to recognise gender equality as a fact of life in our society. Teachers today will have to step up and volunteer to argue against gender discrimination and narrow-mindedness. By this the respondents and the author hope that the fundamentals of gender equality will be accorded and integrated into the legal and social framework of society.

Role of Parents and Family

Home is the first school and mother is the first teacher. The educated women are now conscious of their rights. They become a force to be reckoned with and will soon become equal to men in every field of life. The new millennium, it is hoped, will prove to be a good welcome and blessing for the Indian women! Parents cannot afford to spend on their children's education and when they have to choose between the education of their sons and that of their daughters, they prefer to spend on the education of their sons which they consider more important from the economic point of view. There is a general unwillingness on the part of the parents to spend money for the daughter's education. A boy is required to earn for his living and therefore, it is necessary to educate him. On the other hand the girl is not required to earn for her living as her function in life is to marry and set up a home and bring up a family. Parents do not think that education is necessary for a girl in order that she may fulfil her function as a wife and a mother well. Such domestic education she is supposed to get at home from her mother. It is, therefore, not surprising to find parents reluctant to spend money on their daughter's education, and the same feeling seems to be reflected in the Government of India or the provincial government of this country which have treated the education of girls in a stepmotherly manner.[6] The girls were considered as a burden on their parents until they were married.

Women often see themselves as being at war with the existing order of things. These dilemmas were expressed by cent per cent respondents and said that these can be resolved by address of the problems in a holistic manner. This means that a woman needs choices at different life stages to meander smoothly and ultimately fulfil her larger objective without being constrained by any of the factors, be they familial, social or organisational. There are numerous women who pull out of high profile jobs owing to their responsibilities towards their family. Family or pregnancy puts a brake on women's accelerating careers. Ailing elderly parents at home also prompt women to quit their jobs. In a society like ours, a woman is supposed to look after the whole family—her husband, children and in-laws—whereas men keep away from these responsibilities by just looking after their own jobs.

Now, we have to ask ourselves again and again: Is this not too demanding for women? It is unbelievable, but true, that in spite of all these high demands, women are performing well and balancing all their responsibilities. One wonders how much better a woman can perform and outpace man, if she were given the liberty of performing a single job. Education will help women always know better than others who do not have access to education. They will be more aware of what is happening around them and also in understanding the impact of the environment on their lives. They will know the broad economic structure irrespective of their social background. We will find such women in all walks of life. Given an opportunity such women will excel in their own business as they will know how to convert an opportunity to their own advantage. Family pressures and societal pressures to succeed are equal in both the cases as for educated and uneducated women. It is that feeling of deprivation which is the root cause for feeling that someone else's way of life is better.

Moreover parents must change their attitude to their children and bring them up in a way that reflects equality. Daughters must be given opportunities to develop their decision-making skills and leadership capacities, and sons must be taught to respect their sister as equal. In particular, daughters must have equal access to the same quantity, quality and type of education as sons. The education system must be transformed to ensure that the content and process of education reflect gender equality.

Role of Women

The role of women was limited and restricted to home life, especially looking after children their husbands, and elders. Women themselves then were slow to seek public roles. They should not be perturbed by petty disturbances in and around their lives. An introspection to this end will help them know whether they are fit to start something on their own. Generating a new idea and nurturing it till it becomes a viable and physically identifiable object developed with the might of the mind is what I call a mindset. The ability to start from scratch is the key to success and one needs to have confidence in one's own ideas. Awareness and the need for education is increasing among the Indian women, with a huge potential for growth.

Respondents were of the opinion that the aim of every woman should be to take control of her own and fellow women's careers. One has to steer one's career towards the achievement to one's own satisfaction. Shashi Bhatnagar quoted a saying that "Greatness lies not in being strong, but in the right use of strength." The Chinese philosopher, Confucius, said: "Do what you like, and you'll have a hobby, enjoy your work and its fruits." We used to feel that the place for women was at home. Now we're seeing that they are equal partners and have fabulous leadership potential. The Author sees the ratio of men and women leaders changing significantly in the future.

Development with equality cannot be achieved until such time as women themselves are able to identify the specific problems they face, and to coordinate the demands at the local, state and national level. Women should establish their own identity and respect their own individuality by believing in their capabilities and also by acknowledging the presence of their own species in relation to the society by being bold and determined. Women must develop leadership training and opportunities for all women and encourage them to take leadership roles both as students and as adults in civil society and improve their peripheral vision.

The Universal Declaration of Human Rights states that everyone has the right to take part in the government of his/her country. The empowerment and autonomy of women and the improvement of women's social, economic and political status is essential for the achievement of both transparent and accountable government, and administration and sustainable development in all areas of life. The power relations that prevent women from leading fulfilling lives operate at many levels of society, from the most personal to the highly public. Achieving the goal of equal participation of women and men in decisionmaking will provide a balance that more accurately reflects the composition of society, and is needed in order to strengthen democracy and promote its proper functioning.

It was argued by each and every respondent that women have a very high sense of responsibility when compared to other people of their own age. If the self-motivation level is higher among women who might have had to endure hard times they will work harder and in a more disciplined manner and ensure that they derive high level of commitment. This will make them come through only because of their high level of self-motivation. N. Vaghul, Chairman of ICICI Bank, substantiates this when he says: "Twelve out of 20 top people at ICICI Bank may be women, but they have risen to their positions not because they are women, but because they are talented." The equitable distribution of power and decisionmaking at all levels is dependent on attitudes of women themselves, governments and others involved in women cause undertaking statistical gender analysis and mainstreaming a gender perspective in policy development and the implementation of programmes.

Role of NGOs

The institution of democracy rests on three major pillars: government, business community and civil society. Globalisation is a new initiative offering tremendous potential and scope for enhancing part of civil society in governance. Globalisation can be understood and defined mainly in two ways. One is the economic, the other is the non-economic which broadly includes socio-cultural, historical and political dimension of globalisation, although the economic argument of globalisation appears stronger and widespread than other aspects of cultural globalisation as is generally done in the existing literature on globalisation. Economic, scientific and cultural relations are a way of helping us get to know each other better. There is a close, though not an automatic, link between economic growth and poverty reduction.

Both of these cannot be separated from each other, and it is difficult to observe cultural dimension of globalisation and economic dimension of globalisation independently. Globalisation can be used as a tool for intensifying worldwide social relations which link distant localities in such a way that those local events are shaped by events many miles distant. It could analyse various issues in an integrated manner and take holistic views, rather than a limited sectoral approach. This would help create a new beginning in consonance with the people.

The world is marked by diversity of culture. Every country has the right to choose its own political system and path to development. The community must help the country to eliminate poverty and cooperation on as to achieve common prosperity. There is no universally accepted definition of civil society. Civil society can be said to be a concept of economic and political life of any country. It is universally agreed that participation of the individuals and the institutions engaged in political and economic activities through non-profit organisations whether in the public or private sector are called civil society organisations. Civil society working together with government strengthens the process of building values and norms on the basis of equality.

We are living in a new world, which is more open, complex, diverse and interconnected than ever before. It is information, values, and ideas that are being exchanged in the global era. Civil society is not only diverse and complex but is deeply divided on political and several other issues. "The allegation is made that citizen activism threatens to undermine democratic systems by 'short-circuiting' established procedures for decisionmaking. This is a critique that we in civil society vehemently reject. An active, engaged citizenry is essential for a healthy democratic society. We must resist the notion that elections equal democracy, that a victory at the ballot box is a blank check to rule without any interface and dialogue with citizens in between election periods. To reduce democracy to the singular act of voting once every four or five years is clearly an error. Civic activism complements democratic practices and makes them more effective by drawing citizens more fully into public life and providing a constant check on official accountability" (World Bank Presidential Fellows Lecture Dr Kumi Naidu, Secretary General & CEO,CIVICUS: World Alliance for Citizen Participation Presented at the World Bank headquarters in Washington, DC, 10 February 2003). The interaction between civil society and the government can only be properly understood within this broader frame of action. This is a prerequisite for the socio-economic development of all developing countries including ours. There is no alternative to democracy but civil society working together with government increases the national resources invested in social development and strengthens the country's actions on global issues through argument and debate.

The social norms, cultural beliefs, and the fabric of social interaction are the main ingredients of globalisation of culture, and can be spread through globalisation of knowledge. Ordinary people, caught in the humdrum of life, often wonder whether they can ever balance the needs in order to counter the forces of disruption, hunger, unemployment and other evils in the country, and to promote universal well-being, rapid strides have to be made in the understanding. Necessary measures consistent with the national laws and rules and obligations should be taken to remove impediments and enhance cooperation, which is not only to mutual benefit but also in the broader interest of people and government. They can be strengthened through the promotion in culture, education, science and technology, media, youth and people-to-people relations. Priority should be given to enhancing representation of the deprived class to enhance mutual understanding and trust between the governments, leaders and people to mark a new step forward in strengthening the all-round cooperation in the country.

To induce confidence in the global community in the present context we are now witnessing a new commitment by creating public awareness and ensuring compliance with rules is the solution for a majority of problems, which are becoming complex due to ineffective coordination among enforcing agencies. the populace and institutions involved. Integrity and hard work as two qualities along with consistent efforts are the essential requirements to achieve success. There is need to mobilise activists in the civil society, especially among the groups such as bar councils of districts, teachers, human rights organisations, women, chambers of commerce and industry, labour unions, youth and others. It should be used optimally for strategic inputs. This can come from awareness campaigns by identifying way to sort out shortcomings. Issues related to the development of the community are to be discussed. Efforts should now concentrate on identifying the problems related to regulations and through a mass contact programme, people should be made aware. The use of capability would involve new ways of thinking, change in organisational role and responsibilities and a better understanding of how to create, share and exploit awareness.

Diverse social and infrastructural needs must be addressed more or less simultaneously to ensure a nation's future growth and prosperity. The belief is that continued expansion and intensification of economic cooperation is essential for strengthening relations which provides an important foundation and offers broad prospects for further enhancing international relations. The sustained economic and social development is vital for ensuring peace and stability, which is conducive not only to development, but also to prosperity. Enhance the positive factors of globalisation by fully utilising the substantial potential and opportunities for deepening mutually cooperation to promote the socio-economic development and prosperity. It is vital to understand the role of culture and collective benefits designing a better and more appropriate economic policy. Cultural globalisation will be helpful in growing awareness that we are all part of one human family, sharing the earth as our common home as nature doesn't understand national borders. We all should be committed to develop cooperation on the basis of mutual respect for each other's concerns and equality. We must abide to promote a long-term constructive and cooperation mechanism to strengthen coordination, which will greatly enhance mutual understanding and expand relations. The differences should not be allowed to affect the overall development relations. It is possible to have difference without allowing them to damage mutual relations. There is need to broaden and deepen exchanges which will help enhance and deepen the mutual understanding and trust, for this purpose commitment to work together to maintain tranquillity. Mingled with different strata of society, the perpetual hostility towards some sections of society is deeply embedded in the psyche of people. This is a thing of the past and fundamental changes in the mindset of various sections of society could make an important difference in the lives of thousands. There is a discernible change in the attitude of the people and there is more consistency in their approach. The ideal cannot be sustained unless grounded consciously, and managed adequately and appropriately.

To identify new areas of promise and draw up a comprehensive prospective plan for further economic interaction, impart a fresh momentum to the comprehensive cooperation in the process, we have to go much further to realise our full potential; for this we must first and foremost bridge the information gap. While government, capable of coping with its major problems—problems of water provision, sanitation, transportation, or maintenance of health—can work to address these infrastructural problems, it is for the community to optimise their utilisation. There is no reason to doubt that we will achieve an extraordinary target. Civil society has become important channel for delivery of social services and implementation of development initiatives. It often represents the most effective alternative for delivering social services to low-income communities. It has important role in improving the working of the local self-government department along with the local bodies for achieving the goal of providing better civic amenities to citizens and setting the stage for the massive development. The government's decentralisation programmes which transfer power to the local level (panchayati raj system) will also be helpful in local government-civil society partnerships for service delivery. Civil societies are involved in delivering a wide range of basic services in such areas as village water systems, re-construction efforts, operating schools, housing, sanitation development, transportation and communication. With improvement and more widespread communication facilities, the people can more fully interact with people in other parts of the country. The opportunity for people to communicate or interact in a digital environment whilst being physical located elsewhere has given many people new opportunities in life. So is there something intrinsically "digital about our present hypermodern culture. They share the basic objective and work in the same direction based on the objective of providing services to common people. It should be understood that civil society involvement in service provision is not intended to undermine the role of government, but rather to complement and improve government action and share their experiences in solving development problem as there would be a crisis in the coming decades in energy, drinking water and environmental protection. Citizens of the developing nations have may challenges before them, and to ensure success you take care of the basic needs of the people and accelerate the pace of the nation's growth process.

Civil society plays a critical role in independently reviewing the successes and shortfalls in the implementation of programmes meant for the people and has the ability to channellise the people. It plays the role of broadening governance by increasing the involvement of people and NGO's in decisionmaking by enhancing their capacity to participate effectively in the decisionmaking processes. It is claimed that high performance would accrue due to the adoption of the above innovative solution and the continuity would be achieved through and by providing reinforcement. With the launching of massive and upgradation programmes by the centre and state governments, to develop and adopt new and innovative techniques for economical suffering touching all aspects of our lives individually and socially would be removed. But unfortunately these inventions and techniques have not been put to proper and effective use to caution the local population so as to mitigate the devastating effects. However, good governance can mitigate the effect on our society. Hence, the expectations of people have risen high and is being considered as a measure of good governance.

It is a daunting task for a ordinary person to take stock of the strength of the system and a key measure in the effectiveness would be the integration of civil society initiatives with the system which will ensure stability and transparency in all policies. The government will have to work hard to restore the lost faith of the civil society on those in power in the wake of the unmindful reform programme initiated in the country. These programmes are to be monitored at the highest level, it would be ensured that proper standard was maintained by the field agencies with proper supervision at the ground level. This will be an effort to reach out to these weaker sections of the society and ensure basic civic amenities to them in the areas where they are living.

Civil society creates more opportunities to expand individuals and their personality and helps them just have to be themselves. We are living in a different age; our aspirations are different; our needs are different. Women are not as vulnerable as we think, nor as foolish. Ineffective citizenry that fails to utilise the rights they are entitled have helped in a constructive attempt to find a solution, and empower ordinary citizens to use the right to information as a powerful weapon. It helps build a qualitatively new relationship and mutual desire in developing wider and closer cooperation and understanding in regional and national affairs with a view to deepening coordination on regional and national issues.

Civil society and globalisation have helped ordinary people widen their perspective and providing fresh insight on issues concerning their lives. The trend increasingly is towards better communication and healthy interaction. Civil society is the organisation through which people put forth their concerns, develop and harness their own approaches to pursue policy change. The ways through which civil society interacts with the people and influences governance are also diversified, ranging from advocacy and public protest with different private agencies and organisations. Women nowadays show their capacity of organisation and mobilisation with full use of the information technologies to express themselves through the civil society. It is universally acclaimed that development cannot be sustainable and long lasting unless civil societies' and women's participation is made central to the development process. There is a growing opinion that civil society is all important for strengthening democracy by providing analysis of governance with a systematic understanding of public, private, and mixed arrangements and making politicians accountable to their people and nation.

The social, economic and political problems of women are hindrance to the development. These are also the main reasons for the dissatisfaction of the women with their leadership. Civil society and globalisation have instilled a new national and regional identities and quality of life rank higher among the priorities and suggest what could be the various solutions that government eventually can accept or present towomen as possible alternatives with flexibility. The government should work to strengthen the NGO's, with an emphasis on assisting civil society and empowering women to move toward a more explicit social change through participation in democratic decision making and social movements. New partnership between the civil society and the governments will make for more informed decision making with more transparency, in turn leading to accountability and responsibility. Without this, the vision to have a decentralised set-up will not take off. Our commitment to ensure proper roads, power, drinking water, telephones, educational facilities and healthcare to everyone of India's women will bring hope to them who were victims of indifference. Every effort should be made to work for the common objective and we need to work hard on the front. Globalisation evolves a suitable mechanism to integrate it with the operational activities. It will provide specific techniques aimed at addressing concerns encompassing strategic tactical and operational issues which are cocooned within the boundaries of the social evils like corruption, hunger and fear from society. It is not the masses but only some intellectuals and politicians who get embroiled in corruption. If we see change both in tone and behaviour then a new situation will develop.

References

1. Maithili Vishwanathan, *Development Orientation of Women's Education*, Printwell, Jaipur, 1994. p. 69.
2. Madhuru R. Shah, *Challenges to Higher Education in a Changing India*, Forum of Free Enterprise, Mumbai, 1985, p.2

3. Anindata Mukharji and Neelam Verma, *Socio-Economic Backwardness in Women*, Ashish Publishing House, New Delhi, 1987, p. 18.
4. Uttam Kumar Singh, *Women's Education*, Commonwealth Publishers, New Delhi, 1997, p. 207.
5. *Social Action*, Vol. 52, No. 4, Oct-Dec. 2002, p. 374.
6. Vishwanathan, op. cit., p.63.

9

Suggestions

Brief Starting

Since time immemorial, women have been discriminated against in every aspect of life. They have been at the receiving end for centuries for some reason or the other, but not anymore. Many have signed off women as dreamers. Dreams and fantasies have been ascribed as the domain of women. It is said that for women, private fantasies and illusions serve as a form of resistance to the harsh realities of this materialistic world. Today's women are more assertive, much more determined and even more tactful in handling crises both management and personal. "Women's empowerment and their full participation on the basis of equality in all spheres of society, including participation in the decision-making process and access to power, are fundamental for the achievement of equality, development and peace."[1]

Women can equally play that game with greater efficiency and effectiveness but there is no strong sustainable high growth because their entity lacks the power to influence. They dare to dream big, they build castles in the air, but they also build strong foundations beneath. The present-day women have emerged as winners and have proved that they are better equipped to take on challenges. The play the role of the daughter, the wife, the mother, the professional and the politician who give equal importance to their families as well as their career. They have proved their mettle in enormous professions, be it the media, management, astronomy, administration, defence, sports, beauty, astrology or politics. These days they occupy coveted positions across a wide spectrum of all occupations. Today's woman is an iconoclast, defying all rules whatsoever. Today, she goes not by the book, but rather sets her own rules in this male-dominated world. Women have taken on men in their own areas; of influence and have even beaten them in many areas, it is now in politics that they outdo the men with their efficiency, attitude and intuition. The world has finally sat up and taken notice of woman power, unleashed in its full fury. Success stories are abundant in the field of politics. Sarojini Naidu, Kamala Nehru, Indira Gandhi, Margaret Thatcher, Condoleeza Rice, Sirimavo Bhandarnaike, Golda Myer and Benazir Bhutto to name a few are all women of substance who have made their unique mark in this world. These women are icons and have been a mammoth source of inspiration to millions of women across the world, irrespective of the geographical and demographic barriers. We sincerely believe, the future belongs to women. These women leaders have climbed the ladder by sheer determination, grit and courage. It is high time that the society wakes up to recognise the indomitable spirit of the women, who have reached the top of the political ladder, taking all the hurdles in their stride. These women not only serve as role models and icons of success, but are also a beacon of hope for the coming generation.

The question has always been open to criticism whether women should be kept at arm's length from politics or they should be allowed to take an active part in politics. There are many questions that come in minds of today's leaders: Why should now all this matters? Why is there so much excitement now? What are the contours of such a shift and is it sustainable? We must understand that in this age of political advancement and awakening, the woman's life in itself has been a politics for the last many years. Moreover, every woman has some inspirations and some sentiments. These inspirations and sentiments can only be given a practical shape if they are allowed to enter politics. The question that remains unsettled is the shape and kind of politics.

There have been numerous challenges for women in the past and there will be more in the future and all these will help them perform better. They choose to be loving, peaceful, joyous, harmonious, prosperous, and patient with others and themselves and they have the power to be whatever they want to be. The key factor is that they have the responsibility but not the authority.

"Equality in political decisionmaking performs a leverage function without which it is highly unlikely that a real integration of the equality dimension in government policymaking is feasible. In this respect, women's equal participation in political life plays a pivotal role in the general process of the advancement of women. Women's equal participation in decisionmaking is not only a demand for simple justice or democracy but can also be seen as a necessary condition for women's interests to be taken into account. Without the active participation of women and the incorporation of women's perspective at all levels of decision-making, the goals of equality, development and peace cannot be achieved."[2] Women should be given an opportunity to demonstrate their budding political influence. They know that may seem like a tough one to some people, and even possibly blasphemous. They must be allowed to understand their problems and they should have a full say in making those problems solved in the right way. If they are debarred from doing so, it would mean nipping in the bud the political awakening that is mutual in every heart.

Modern critics who are of opinion that women should be kept away from politics forget that our society within organic concepts can only advance. The women are also a part of our society that is our body. Any organ of the body which is undeveloped makes the body cripple and infirm. Social science affirms that a woman's place in society marks the level of civilisation. Thus we can assume that for the betterment of the society, of the welfare of the community, for the prosperity of the nation and for every lasting peace in the universe, the women should be allowed to have their say in all matters, which concern them. Empowerment is not something that can be given; it must be taken. Those (men) who have it, and want to share it, can provide the conditions and the language, which make it possible for those who are in need of it, to approach it fearlessly. It is up to leadership to bring in the right team of skilled individuals. Empowerment also supports the country's implementation of its strategy and is all about seeing a group of motivated people brought together with the same objectives. It is the society that should decide the 'responsibilities' to be taken up by women, unlike the situation now where the men define their responsibilities towards the society and women are equipped with the authority, to make things happen.

The politicians should remember that the coming generation would never pardon them if they will not allow women to take an active part in politics and in all those matters which are concerned with their present and future. Women should not follow the slogans and the dogmas of the so-called politicians who proclaim themselves to be their friends, well-wishers and their saviours. In practical life, the woman is judged by man's law, as if she were a man, not a woman. There is a general tendency to focus on the negatives. One lone individual's character can make a difference in his or her circle of influence and we can all see women as catalysts both at home and at work. We are seeing energy and enthusiasm among women, absolutely new freshness in them and witnessing something positive. It lays the foundation for better decisionmaking and communication. This is very positive phenomenon and we earnestly hope that there will be a great deal of care taken if we want this to get through and become a reality.

It becomes increasingly important to acknowledge their efforts and reward them for the same. The right person can contribute positively towards the achievement of the goals. It is a fair play of competency and whoever is more competent wins. Goals can never be achieved until everyone thinks critically about what must be done differently and then does it. When you allow people to innovate, be ready to tolerate mistakes. It can go wrong, so mistakes are bound to happen. It has become imperative due to the change. Life is a continuous risk. Without risks and mistakes, there is no learning, no change and no gain. Winston Churchill said, "A pessimist sees the difficulty in every opportunity; an optimist sees the opportunity in every difficulty." Learning from our mistakes is part and parcel of the process of growing. They have the ability to learn and acquire them. Unless policies and strategies are converted into actions, their sole purpose will be to decorate written constitution, law books, government gadgets and nothing else.

Both media and political leaders more likely to have positive attitude and have a substantial role to play in bridging the space. The divide can definitely be bridged and this can only be bridged through political decisions using the people's rights. It is important for the leaders to go through every introspection to realise the full potential of women.

The most important node in holstering this process is a shift in public perceptions but all this needs to be maintained with care, and government and personal support is necessary. This is the chance to show that the community has matured and can translate that into political effectiveness. The current mood of optimism could change quickly if the new dispensation does not deliver.

Political parties hesitate to send women parliament and legislative assemblies, but women can be successful like their male counterpart. It is attributed that economic development of any country is associated with country's political leadership. Experiences suggest that the role of woman has become an important part of country's economic growth. However, it was only in recent times that many countries have started addressing the issues of women seriously. It has become a well known fact that women possess a unique skill; they encourage participation; they make people feel important, included and energised; they share power and information. This skill needs to be utilised in the politics of the future.

Traditionally, whenever political parties developed a pool of potential candidates, they excluded women. However, country's politics can no longer afford to limit their pool of talented human resources by excluding a particular group just based on gender. It is actually the political parties that always find it difficult to select women for tickets in parliament and legislative assemblies. They are so prejudiced against women that they are certain that female leaders will not succeed in managing effectively even if sent. Some parties are hesitant because of the insurmountable dual-career issues as leader and family caretaker.

The avowed objective of political parties should be to stimulate awareness and to enhance political attention and action oriented strategies about women's participation in politics. Peter F. Drucker said, "Effective leadership is not about making speeches or being liked; leadership is defined by results not attributes." The basic principles should be to preserve, protect and promote social harmony ensure in a sustained manner the welfare and well-being of women and to fully empower them politically, this will help us gauge the health of India's democracy.

Gender bias is a worldwide phenomenon, but it is especially pernicious in the Third World, where most of women's activities take place for the purpose of household consumption. With a hue and cry for gender equality, this powerful and perfectionist male image and resulting suppressed emotional needs, have also started targeting women. On one side, women have become more hardworking, educated, loyal, dedicated and responsible, on the other, the dual role of housewives and career women imposes a great strain on them.

Despite women's increased percentage in higher education, their greater commitment to politics as a career and equal opportunity legislation, women leaders in every country remain a small fraction of those in higher positions in politics. The leaders are of the opinion that women could never live up to the expectations of the people in taking country to the heights aspired. Most political parties are reluctant to select women as leaders. Some of the political parties continue to resist the prospect of parting with 33 per cent seats for women in the legislative assemblies and parliament. Only 44 women of the 355 women who contested have been elected in the Lok Sabha elections with the highest number – seven – MPs coming from Uttar Pradesh alone. The highest number of women contestants, 62, were also from Uttar Pradesh from where the Bill is facing resistance from the ruling Samajwadi Party.

It is the actions not the lip service that really matters. The two main political parties claiming to be champions for women's reservation – the Congress and the BJP—gave the party ticket to 45 and 30 women, respectively. There were as many as 117 women candidates who did not contest under any political banner. The remaining tickets were given by the smaller political parties. "Take measures, including, where appropriate, in electoral systems that encourage political parties to integrate women in elective and non-elective public positions in the same proportion and at the same levels as men; Protect and promote the equal rights of women and men to engage in political activities and to freedom of association, including membership in political parties and trade unions; Review the differential impact of electoral systems on the political representation of women in elected bodies and consider, where appropriate, the adjustment or reform of those systems."[3] This clearly suggest the magnitude of the problems we are facing cannot be subdued because politicians prefer not to address the problem if they can possibly avoid it. History might eventually reveal that the anti-women attitude is among the greatest threats to sustainable development and the future of humankind.

What we learn from the experiences is that the more you put yourself in a winning position, the more you are likely to win. The higher Self can be a wonderful guide and it will certainly give you the confidence and the platform for the bigger stage. Society is changing rapidly and being a perfect politician is no longer an exclusive male privilege. Women leaders, all over the world, are taking over in a big way. They are no longer content to work in the traditional position of teachers, receptionists and family caretakers. Women will have to understand that there is just a small opening for opportunity and it will be closing rather rapidly if they do not grab it for there is not a moment to lose. Political leaders have an important role to play in addressing these challenges. The good news is that political parties seem to be realising that they can no longer ignore these issues.

Women power has been grossly underrated. The women may not be highly qualified but their wisdom cannot be doubted; they may not be physically very strong but their mental strength and readiness to work hard speak volumes about their character; finally, they may be inhibited leaders but their extraordinary skills and interpersonal abilities cannot be doubted. They represent a major force, a dormant volcano, a repository of immense potential and abilities. Empowerment of women through education, economic freedom and political leadership can lead to the revolutionary era of development of human resource. Women will feel a sense of belonging towards the people and nation and this will form the key for the success. Our leaders have to first understand the perceptions, values, beliefs of the people and when we create awareness in the minds of women and educate them about the same, it will have a great effect. This particular strategy should be used and there is need to educate the people and women about the importance of this issue.

For years, women were content with whatever treatment and services they had across to and were offered to them. The advent of media, television in particular, has created awareness in the minds of women. Increasing literacy rate and media penetration have laid the foundation for change in the behaviour of people towards women. The effects of globalisation have finally reached the people of India. The changing face of globalisation has not only transformed the lives of general people, but has also had its effect on the women mindset. Women are no longer the same, they now need more than what they wanted earlier. There is sea change in the attitudes, lifestyles and preferences of women. This behavioural change in the attitudes of women has indeed forced politician and leaders to give a serious thought about women's issues.

We can all say to our leadership what Winston Churchill said, "Attitude is a little thing that makes a big difference," and Christina W. Baum said, "Perspective is everything; change your perspective and you change reality."

Concluding Observations and Suggestions

There is a certain ethical know-how to survive and flourish in any situation and environment. It appears that politics in our lives is a fact we all have to live with. We learn the system, and work round it when we can. To be able to determine the requirements of each situation and each person one faces, and to select just the right approach to make things work, and necessarily in a manipulative way, is the nature of a politically savvy person. One must be friendly and helpful person, good at building relationships, in the process of building relationships, one must make himself and his work visible. Being visible is a very important skill and a mark of political savvy. All these contributed to his getting ahead. One must be politically astute and realistic about the nature of human beings and while at the same time must believe in ethics and values. This helps one move upwards without necessarily compromising one's principles. It is possible to put one's career on the fast track by practising positive politics. The one who gets ahead is the one who walks the middle road. The politically astute are skilled at reading the power structures—who the decision-makers are—and then, act upon these.

We must give women opportunity to work at every level when they are consciously making the effort to develop. It is affirmed that humans are born equal, that they are entitled to equality of opportunity, and this principle should be practised.

Take the initiative to its logical end and it would "transform" the life of the women. This factor will play a very crucial role and give them sense of participation. Mary Kay Ash says, "Don't limit yourself. Many people limit themselves to what they think they can do. You can go as far as your mind lets you. What you believe, remember, you can achieve." This is a democratic leap forward that will elevate women's status, which despite a late start could finally make it.

The study revealed that parents of high income, small family structure, higher education and occupation at all levels favoured their daughters going to school. "There has been an impressive growth in the area of higher education with an increase in annual student enrolment from 7.26 million in 1997-98 to 9.95 million in 2003-04. Enrolment of women students rose from 2.45 million in 1997-98 to 4.03 million in 2004-05, constituting 40.22 per cent of the total enrolment."[4] Parents of both the schoolgoing girls and dropout girls expressed dissatisfaction towards the prevailing school conditions. The socio-economic conditions are more conclusive to schoolgoing girls than to dropout girls.

Adequate and quality women's education is considered as an essential prerequisite for economic independence of women. It will lead them to improve job knowledge and skills and will also be helpful in eliminating fear in attempting new tasks. It will help them prepare new, relevant guidelines for work. It is a proven aid in encouraging and achieving self-development and self-confidence. It will boost the morale of women, goodwill and better image of women. It will help women in identifying with government's mission, objectives, policies, it will also help in fostering authenticity, openness and trust among women. Education will create appropriate climate for growth in communication and provide information on equal opportunity and affirmative action among women. Education will be helpful in providing information to women for future needs of self and society and will provide a good climate for learning, growth and coordination. It will eliminate suboptimal behaviour in women, and will internalise and operationalise motivational variables of recognition, achievement, growth, responsibility and advancement.

Education is a mission to inspire fresh thinking and is encouraging innovative thinking through out the life and a proactive integrating innovation and innovative thinking into everyday life. Education is a mission in handling conflict, thereby helping to prevent stress and tension and will also be helpful in developing leadership skill, motivation, loyalty, better attitudes, improved interpersonal skills. It is now time to rethink, reframe and refocus our efforts to ensure that education is indeed integrated throughout all aspects of our lives. Education can no longer be confined to select people. The government and leaders must ensure that support to women are in place to encourage them in broad participation and action.

We are not talking about the typical housemaid who can only wash and clean but with the increasing availability of choices and exposure to the good things of life, women have shortly undergone a drastic change. It is felt that the education imparted to these homes was extremely regressive. If they get specialised training this will play important part in imparting values in developing the better survival skills against the vagaries of competitive way of life.

Many problems arise from poor implementation of plans despite being well thought out and articulated. The ground reality execution of these policies are going to have an impact on the overall development of the country. Framing of desired curriculum is needed for effective education system and to achieve these objectives and aims of the curriculum, psychology of the education have to be considered, W. B. Yeats rightly says that "education is not the filling of pail but the lighting of fire."[5] All officials must act within the confines of the authority invested with them and it is their duty to make and enact informed decisions and policies in the best interests of the public. All officials shall conduct their activities, on behalf of the government and public with honesty, integrity and fairness. All officials will act in good faith, responsibly, with due care, competence and diligence, without allowing their independent judgement to be subordinated. Officials are required to comply with all applicable laws, rules and regulations, both in letter and in spirit. In order to assist the government in promoting lawful and ethical behaviour, officials must report any possible violation of law, rules, regulation or the code of conduct to the society. Any code should be widely and transparently communicated to be effective. All the officials in senior or junior position must receive a copy of the code. Everyone must understand the importance of compliance and the consequences of not complying. Deliberate failure to comply with the standards required must be met by appropriate disciplinary action. A disciplinary system should be adopted so that all concerned are aware that deviations from established procedures would be dealt with in a fair, transparent and effective manner.

Education directed towards human understanding and good will, the safeguarding of dignity and freedom, and respect for human dignity. A majority of women prefer to choose or are ordered to choose domestic work over work for market.[6] Rising living standard and poverty reduction across the globe are to a great extent the result of education and technological advances. Voluntary professional organisations of teachers should be treated as partners in educational development.[7] Benjamin Disraeli declared long ago, "Upon the education of the people of this country, the fate of this country depends." Therefore all progressive countries invest the best of their resources for education. Global education conference for at Jomtien–Bangkok boldly launched Education For All In 1990.[8] These include data collection and monitoring, target setting, the provision of women-friendly working conditions, fair and transparent recruitment procedures, confidence building and awareness-raising will be supported through the appropriate training programmes. These qualities can effectively help tackle the seemingly intractable and the most formidable of problems and can influence the government to move in the right direction. The support will go a long way towards enabling to clear the problems in this region and improve the lives of a large numbers of people. So how do you bring about change, real change?

Women will have to make many adjustments in their life and will have to do things differently so that they can improve. We genuinely believe that the desired outcomes are difficult but not impossible. We all know it would be a very difficult but their confidence and education will make it. If they just try to stand up and show that they aren't scared or have no fear, they have a chance to prove their worth. Only education can get them this far and is way up there as well because it opens up a lot of avenues. Once Nelson Mandela said, "Education is the most powerful weapon of change the world." Education has been the driving force behind many recent developments. Women would be looking for amelioration of the situation which would dispel some of the concerns that they are experiencing today, suppression of the elementary democratic rights of women. This will become reality if we don't place unreasonable burden on women. The government must assess and spell out a policy, identify the targets and problem areas and detail a strategy, which will have to be adopted. The government's efforts are being undertaken in a piecemeal and casual manner.

Sexual harassment at workplace violates a person's sense of dignity and right to earn a living with dignity. It is against the fundamental rights embodied in the Indian Constitution and also against basic human rights. A mechanism has to be set up for addressing that problem and give it more focus and emphasis. All is not lost. The major challenge to the humanities today is in exploring the radically novel and critical ways of relating or associating the human articulations. We need to redouble our efforts to ensure a sensible and sensitive approach. What this means is that some changes may be called for in the principles. It is indeed this relating or connecting that will underwrite what it is to be human in the coming years.

The role given to women in whatever capacity would definitely benefit them in thinking they are better or equal to others. Implement the welfare scheme sincerely and the women should be integrated in the society and should not be discriminated again. The government is responsible for implementing the programme in the form of regularising giving technical expertise and coordinating the works of various NGOs working for the betterment of women. They should get together and discuss the condition of women and the possible solution to their woes. Women are not a charity case anymore. Education has promised to them to take control of their lives and to realise their full potential. There are vast male-female differences in the choice of quantum and type of education, specialisation, nature and intensity of work, occupation and job. Consequently there are vast earning differences based on gender, in nature and place of both developed as well as less developed countries. However, the differences are very stark in India and other developing countries. More women are now getting education and working outside the home for income so much so that in developing countries they have almost reached the level attained by their male counterpart but there is still wide gender segregation. Occupational fields are often dominated by one gender. Female-dominated occupations are given lower salaries as compared to male-dominated occupations in spite of similar education or skill level required. Development programmes are also not unbiased on the subject of gender.

Education will leverage women's skills and knowledge and make effective use of the latest information technology tools to find better ways to serve their country and the people and will reorient them as far as the problems of the people and especially women are concerned by adopting a more open approach. Summer Savon says, "It's becoming apparent that female insights such as connection, introspection, intuition and complexity of relation-ship are more appropriate concepts to describe what we now know about reality." The Constitution of India has given equality of education opportunities irrespective of any type of discrimination including sex. In the post-independent India, it is felt that women's education should be given more importance. It is felt that education of women is essential to achieve the goals of democracy and equality. Women can use knowledge to create sustained competitive advantage and they will generate their own ideas which would then be developed. Education will also incorporate the ability in women to rescue from "false negatives" and prepare them to serve a cause. Five thrust areas viz. adult literacy, primary education, higher education, decentralisation of management of education and technical education, have been identified to achieve universalisation of the elementary education to make education relevant to the needs of the community and also to meet new challenges of liberalisation and globalisation of the economy.[9] Had we implemented this programme diligently, we would have by now eliminated illiteracy.

Steps should also be taken to ensure that the sector which is one of the highest generator of employment in the country provide more job opportunities to women. Cheryl F. says, "A shared responsibility of women leaders on campus is to make their system more receptive to the presence and progress of women as a group." It is a fact that not much attention is paid to the profile of female teachers especially about their academic and professional qualifications and competencies to tackle the complexities of today's education.

A quality education can make the difference between success or failure, and revolves around needs and the individual's preferences to have a work-life balance. Quality education has a powerful role to play for converting human beings into human asset. Now, women are considered as an assets instead of a liability, and the doors of education are open for them. The strategy therefore should be to provide education at all levels and incorporated at an appropriate level, management, administration and entrepreneurial training to our youth, more particularly to girls, in arts and commerce faculties by providing autonomous certificate and diploma courses in these areas which can be completed while they are college-going students. Education is manifestation of divinity already present in man.

1. Value education should be provided to women so that they may be able to guide their children for better life. The process of education as started by NCERT cannot be a value neutral process.
2. They should also be provided job-oriented education to earn specially at the time of necessity and difficulty.
3. Social awareness and mental alertness are also necessary. Her education is not complete unless she is provided with this knowledge.[10]

The government has also been sensitive to the needs of women and has formulated several policies and welfare programmes for the emancipation of them in the country through a large number of economic schemes but these would be absolute transparent.

Education is never finished but has to be continued whole life. Education means the drawing out, or development of the faculties. This begins in school and college; but it does not end there. At school and college one learns the rudiments, and gains a smattering of knowledge on various subjects. More important, one learns there law to learn the best methods of acquiring knowledge. School and college education trains the mind (or should do), and makes it accustomed to continuous application and study. But this is not the whole of education; in a sense, it is but a preparation for education. Our education should never be 'finished' at any rate so far as this life is concerned, until we die.

"Every person," said Gibbon, the historian, "has two educations: one which he receives from others, and one, more important which he gives himself." And Sir Walter Scott confirmed this when he wrote: "The best part of every man's education is that which he gives himself." "That which is put into us by others," says Samuel Smiles, "is always far less than ours that which we acquire by our own efforts. Knowledge conquered by labour becomes a possession a property entirely our own."

If this is so, how do you hope to continue your education when you leave school or college? I say 'plan' for mere hoping will not accomplish much. You must make up your mind to do it, and form some definite plan of studies. First you must keep up your reading. Too many young men close their books when they have taken their degrees, and learn no more. They very soon forget all they have ever learnt. But, if you intend to continue your education, you must find time for serious reading. "Practice, knowledge, again practice, and again, knowledge. This form repeats itself in endless cycles, and with each cycle the content of practice and knowledge rises to a higher level" as Mao Ze Dong sadi. Go on with the subjects, or some of them, you began as a student and take up new ones that you feel will interest you. Further if you have the chance, join continuation classes, attend what lectures you can, become a member of some literary circle or debating society. Solitary study is not enough; you can learn much from discussion and conversation with others. Flexible education, training and retraining programmes for lifelong learning that facilitate transitions between women's activities at all stages of their lives should be created. But, what ever you do, never imagine that your education is 'finished'.

Education must develop in the learner a holistic- integrated personality. In other words, education should create in each pupil confidence, faith, creativity and fearlessness, and it is only through quality teachers and educators at all levels that this can be achieved. How do we ensure global competitiveness and the answer to all such and related questions lie in strengthening first the faculty members of colleges and educational institutions, in a systematic and visionary manner. Hence there is a need for continuous training to teachers also. For making education more effective at all levels, there are only five parameters: these are curriculum development, faculty training, appropriate evaluation pattern, linkages with the society and identity to be given to the

Higher education must empower all concerned to become world class citizens and provide empowerment so as to give dignity to one's profession. A scrutiny reveals that barring a few, most of the universities do not think they have a role beyond awarding degree to students who are willing and able to pay high fees. Indisputably, the faculty member is a key figure in the educational process. Yet not much attention is paid to preparing a faculty member for the job, nor do adequate facilities exist for in-service training. In education, faculty development, or faculty improvement is an overlooked area. The author therefore emphasizes that it is only through education and training that women can be empowered to play their meaningful role in modern times. More and more women should enter the service enterprises, i.e., education, health, banking, insurance, post & communication, travel & transport sectors, etc. and through continuous education and appropriate training they will emerge more 'Synergic' for 'Nation Building Activities'. Training for this purpose can be imparted in smaller groups, through visiting faculty and through project work and viva. Hence expert faculty be made available as visiting staff in schools and colleges along with full time teachers.

A teacher has to be a 'critical thinker, life long learner and a leader of change'. The key to effective leadership lies in acquiring training. It is only on the basis of wisdom and love for the profession that dignity can be brought to our profession. A teacher must have the wisdom and a sense of honour. The real role of a teacher is 'doing' the most challenging work in society – the work of 'making men' and "growing leaders'. A teacher, like an artist, has to shape, enrich and tone the character, wisdom and culture of each individual pupil. The teacher must constantly focus on building up sterling character in our children. The teacher can transform himself for the better by practising human values. Selfless love is the foundation of a happy and harmonious life in a family, community and society and it is the role of a teacher and parent to see that the main source of building the character of future generation is not dried up. You can buy a bed, but not sleep;

you can buy a book, but not brain; you can buy food but not hunger; you can buy clothes, but not beauty; you can buy medicine, but not health; you can buy a house, but not home; you can build a temple, but not divinity. How can we buy all these? With character and sacrifice, one can acquire all these. The teachers have therefore to bring dignity to profession by their own effort.

Education is a potent source of socio-economic and political changes. The government has to take actions to ensure that female teachers and professors have the same opportunities as and equal status with male teachers and professors, in view to support and develop gender studies and research at all levels of education, especially at the postgraduate level of academic institutions. It must apply them in the development of curricula, including university curricula, textbooks and teaching aids, and in teacher training. The government must see that gender equality and cultural, religious and other diversity are maintained and respected in educational institutions. What happened to women through education? Women came out of whatever local, parochial society they happened to have been born in to meet the world with an open mind.

Media

The mass media has not any concerted efforts to discuss serious issues that concern women and prepare the women to plan their rightful and equal role in the society. To change the situation, we will have to regularly monitor that media and point out the merits as well as demands on a continuous basis. Perhaps the women's organisations could create a media-monitoring cell for the purpose. Freedom of expression is a right given to us by the Constitution of India, and if it's available to everybody why should one be denied it? We have to do many things to remove the apprehensions of the women, which have failed to expand for want of proactive policies.

Education will open the gateway for women with the new opportunity and will lead to knowledge of their own right. This will be an awakening of half of India's oppressed citizens and government must work for making education the cornerstone of empowerment. Women may enjoy full citizen rights and be formally equal members of political parties, yet they feel more tolerated than accepted. Media need to cooperate and to help the cause of justice. The media must live up to the role of watchdog to raise awareness, protect basic human rights, and empower communities and specially women if they are to continue enjoying public credibility. Media must take care of the women by helping them to find solutions to their problems and provide an opportunity to demonstrate their budding political influence. Particular attention must be paid to the development of inter-personal communication skills amongst women.

Education will provide opportunities to show that women have matured and can translate that into political effectiveness. There have been numerous challenges and there will be more in the future but all these will help them perform better.

Women's Involvement

Their male counterpart like, father, brother, husband and political leaders as well as male panchayat members should have a soft corner, respect and positive attitude for them. They should not do anything which should discourage them.[11]

Gender Equality

When asked about, how do they see their role in the society now? What is the role of them as women in the future of the state and the real role in politics and local government? What will be their role there? There were questions asked by them in response to: what is democracy? How does it work? What are the rights and responsibilities of citizens? Perhaps much is needed to see things from close quarters to clarify their thinking and to bring the whole issue into clearer focus.

Establish and maintain an award for persons who are working to uphold the values of truth and honesty. Peoples' awareness and cooperation is what will ultimately make this campaign succeed, unless there is public cooperation with the administration, mere declaration will not suffice. Ignorance is the main problem and we could get rid of that just by getting to know each other better and the divide can definitely be bridged. The evidence so far is not definitive enough to call for shift in strategy and fundamental changes must occur in your physical brain, it must learn a new pattern of functioning. Women must be aware of certain awakening principles with the self-realisation that this needs to be put into practice women's education, which can influence their lives. Women's education can shape their minds and help them to determine their destiny forever. They who realise the urgency of the situation and believe in the good, education will give them all the energy they need and for this women have to take care of the situation themselves. They would be well acquainted with the conditions better and handle situations much more efficiently. Education will work as a catalyst to the change that will take place and put their life on the line to ensure that change takes place. They have a right to decide for themselves and it is what will make them mature and responsible adults.

Women need protection from discrimination and some affirmative action to overcome disadvantage and they can lead a reasonably untroubled life of dignity. They will be able to get their voices heard and press for their demands. However they lack a platform to express themselves. They must galvanise their subconscious to forge intuitive, creative and broader perception for resolving the problem. The governing bodies should be forced to face up to their responsibilities in relation to what is happening to the vast majority of citizens, and the community at large must start to recognise and confront the humanitarian issues.

— Finance corporation to sanction liberal loans for women to solve their unemployment problem.

— The media should help the government generate confidence in women and make them understand the problems faced by them.

— Assess and spell out a policy, identify the targets and problem areas and detail a strategy, which will have to be adopted. Democracy would be weakened if the promises were not implemented. The role of various participating organisations should be spelt out and the implementation monitored and the unified approach will make it possible. Bettsey Barhorst says, "We had technical gurus, but it takes politics and persuasion to make things happen." Parliamentarians need to be educated properly about the policies and strategies before they frame laws and political parties should be made accountable.

— Programmes to generate awareness among women at district, state, regional and national level.

— Booklets on law relating to women including constitutional provisions should be published.

— Periodicals magazines, highlighting women problems and their solution, should be published and distributed among the society.

— A moral pressure should be brought by the government on officials to implement existing laws relating to women strictly and honestly and to enact, if necessary, more acts and laws.

— To organise rallies and group meetings in remote areas in rural and urban areas to awaken women for their rights and dignity.

— Girl education should be free at all levels.

References

1. Beijing Declaration.
2. Ibid.
3. Ibid
4. *Economic Survey, 2005-06.*
5. *Social Action,* vol. 52, No. 4, Oct.-Dec., 2002, p.366.
6. *Miracle of Teaching,* Vol. VII, No. 1, Jan-April-2007, p.9.
7. Ibid., p.10.
8. Ibid., p.11.
9. CSR *Year Book 2000,* p. 630.
10. *Miracle of Teaching,* 03, 2006, p. 89.
11. Bhola Nath Gosh, *Rural Women Leadership,* Mohit Publications, New Delhi, 2002, p-103.

Bibliography

Books

Dave, J. K., *A Study of Evolution of Female Education in Gujarat*, 1971.

Gosh Bhola Nath, *Rural Women Leadership*, Mohit Publications, New Delhi, 2002.

Greenberg Edward S. & Benjamin I. Page, *The Struggle for Democracy*, Wesley Educational Publishers Inc. United States, 1999, p.10.

Horton, Paul B., Gerald R. Leslie, *The Sociology of Social Problems*, Princeton-Hall, Inc., United States of America, 1978.

Kuhn Berthold, *Participatory, Development In Rural India*, Radiant Publishers, New Delhi, 1998.

Learner David, *The Passing of Traditional Society, Modernising the Middle East*, The Free Press, New York, 1968.

Mathur, N.N.G., *Problems of Tribal Education*, Shiv Publishers Distributors, Udaipur, 1994.

Max, Weber, *The Theory of Social and Economic Organisation*, Oxford University Press, New York, 1947.

Mehta Arati, *Progressive Women and Political Identity*, Kanishka Publishers, Distributors, New Delhi, 2004.

Milbrath, Laster W., *Political Participation*, Chicago: Rand McNally and Co. , 1965.

Mukharji Anindata and Neelam Verma, *Socio-Economic Backwardness in Women*, Ashish Publishing House, New Delhi, 1987.

Naik, C., *Education of Women in the Province of Bombay (1918-1947)*, 1949.

Papanek, H., *Changing Women in Changing Society*, University of Chicago Press, 1973.

Rai, S. B., *Society and Education in India (1813-1857)*, 1955.

Ramachandran, P., *Women and Education*, Tata Institute of Social Science, 1963.

Riggs, F.W., *Bureaucracy and Political Development* Princeton, N. Univ. Press, 1963.

Roy West and Nicholas, *Understanding Sexual Attacks*, Heinemann Educational Books Ltd., 1978 .

Seltz Clair, *Research Methods in Social Science*, Holt Rinehart and Winston Inc., New York, 1962.

Sen, Sankar, Human Rights and Law Enforcement, Concept Publishing Company, New Delhi, 2002.

Shah, Madhuru R., *Challenges to Higher Education in a Changing India*, Forum of Free Enterprise, Mumbai, 1985.

Shastri, K., *Political Linkage and Rural Development*, National Publishing House, New Delhi, 1976.

Singh Anil Kumar, *Approaches To Tribal Development*, Sarup & Sons, New Dehli, 1994, p.123.

Singh, Uttam Kumar, *Women's Education*, Commonwealth Publishers, New Delhi, 1997, p. 261.

Soni, Jasprit Kaur, *Women Empowerment : Exploring the Facts*, Authorspress, New Delhi, 2006.

Thakur, D.N., *Trabal Women*, Deep and Deep Publication, New Delhi, 1996.

Upadhyay, H. C., *Status Women in India*, Anmol Publications Pvt. Ltd. New Delhi. 1997.

Uphoff, N. T. and Cohen, J, *Feasibility and Application of Rural Development Participation: A State of the Art Paper*, Cornell University, U.S.A., 1979.

Vakil, C.N., *Poverty, Planning and Inflation*, Allied Publishers Pvt. Ltd., Bombay, 1978.

Vidya, K.C., *Political Empowerment of Women at the Grassroots*, Kanishka Publishers Distributors, New Delhi, 1997.

Vishwanathan, Maithili, *Development Orientation of Women's Education*, Printwell, Jaipur, 1994.

Wolfensohn James, in *Voices and Choices at a Macro Level: Participation in Country-owned Poverty Reduction Strategies*, edited by Parmesh Shah and Deborah Youssef, February 2002, World Bank.

Yasin Mohammad* Pradip K. Sengupta, *Indian Politics, Processes, Issues and trends*, Kanishka Publishers, Distributors, New Delhi, 2004.

ARTICLES

Antony, Valsamma, 'Empowering the Urban Women through Micro – Enterprises: A Case Study', *The Economic Challenger*, No. 7, Issue 27, April-June, 2005.

Batt, D. K., *Human Rights and Status of Women : A Socio-Legal Analysis*, A. I. R. 2000 (journal Section), p. 79.

Daymont T. N. and P. J Andrisan, Job Preferences, College Major and the Gender gap in Earnings, *The Journal of Human Resources*, 1984,

Gill S. S. & Ranjit Singh Ghuman, 'Rural Health: Proactive Role for the State', *Economic And Political Weekly*, Vol.XXXV, No.51, December 16-22. 2000.

Hein, Wolfgang, Globalisation and Social Insecurity: International Organisations; *Civil Society And Global Governance*, Clusters - 24 September 2005, 12:13 UTC.

Huntington, Samuel P., Political Development and Political Decay, *World Politics*, Vol. XVIII, No.3, April 1963, p. 388.

Kaur, Jasprit 'Tribal Women: Emerging New Elite', *Tribe*, Vol.31, No.3-4, 1999.

Misra, Jugal Kishore, Empowerment of Women in India, *Indian Journal of Political Science*, Vol. LXVII, No. 4, Oct-Dec., 2006.

Mullojanov, Parviz, Civil Society and Peacebuilding. *Accord*, Vol. 10, March 2001.

Rajagopal, Shobhita & Kanchan Mathur, 'Women Empowerment Through State Benevolence', *Economic And Political Weekly*, Vol.XXXV, No.33, August 12-18, 2000.

Rao, Nitya, 'Education Quality with Quantity', *Economic And Political Weekly*, Vol.XXXV, No.48, November 25-December 1, 2000.

Reddy Kranthi Kumar K. & Vijaya Lakshmi Reddy P., 'Globalisation, Agriculture and Women', *Social Action*, Vol.51, No.4, October-December, 2001.

Sen, Aditya, Major Strides Towards Rural Development, *Kurukshetra*, August 1994.

Seshadri, K., 'The Open Government and Its Enemies', *The Indian Journal of Public Administration*, Vol.XXV, No.4, 1979.

Sharma, K.L., 'Social Structure and Political Change', *The Indian Political Science Review*, Vol.8, 1969.

Shetty Sadanand, (editorial), 'No Time to Pause', *One India One People*, May, 1998.

Singh, M. K., Participation of Women in Economic Development; Trends and Issues, *Indian Journal of Industrial Relations*, 1987.

Singh, Trilok, 'Employment and Planning –Assessment and Strategies in India', *Indian Economic Journal,* April-June 1986.

Smith, Gary and Michael Muetzelfeldt. "Global Governance and Strategies for Civil Society." *Pacifica Review,* 12: 3, October 1, 2000.

UNESCO: *A Dictionary of Social Science,* Edited by Julius Guide and William L. Kolb, 1964, p. 228, Quoted from Durkheim's *Education and Sociology* , Translated by S.D. Fox the Free Press, 1965, pp. 70-71.

Magazines / Journals / Newspafers

Competition Success Year Book, 2001.

Cronicle Year Book, 2002.

Effective Executive, February, 2006.

Indian Highways, Vol. 32, No. 4, April 2004.

Manorama Year Book, 2005.

Miracle of Teaching, Vol. VII, No. 1, Jan-April-2007.

Miracle of Teaching, 03, 2006.

New Women, Vol. 11, Issue 1, January 2007.

Review of Politics, Vol. XIV, No. 1, Jan.-June, 2006.

Social Action, Vol. 52, No. 4, Oct-Dec. 2002.

Sura's Year Book, 2005.

The Economic Challenger, No. 7, Issue 27, April-June, 2005.

Times of India (Daily Newspaper)

The Hindu (Daily Newspaper)

Government Reports and other Documents

Ahuja, Ram, *Research Report on "Awareness of Rights Among Women"*, 1982.

Census of India, Rajasthan, Series-9, Paper-1, Paper-2, Paper-3, 2001.

REPORT: Civil Society Consultations on International Environmental Governance, Nairobi, 22 and 23 May 2001.

Approach Paper to the Tenth Five Year Plan (2002-2007), Planning Commission, The Government of India, New Delhi, September, 2001.

The Tenth Five Year Plan 2002-07; Women and Children; Planning Commission, New Delhi.

Beijing Declaration.

Government of India, *Third Five Year Plan,* Planning Commission, New Delhi.

National Policy for the Employment of Women-2001-India; Department of Women and Child Development, Government of India, *Economic Survey,* New Delhi.

Planning Commission, Government of India, *Draft Fifth Five Year Plan,* 1974-79, New Delhi.

Ninth Five Year Plan Draft, 1997-2002, Planning Commission, Government of India, New Delhi.

Indian Education Commission Report, 1964-1966.

Census of India, 1981, *Series 18,* Part II B, Primary Census Abstract, Rajasthan.

Extract From A Report By National Commission For Women, Education for Tribal Women, *Social Welfare,* Vol. 42 No. 5-6, August-September 1995.

Indian Confederation of Indigenous and Tribal People 3rd General Assembly Meeting, 1997.

National Commission for Scheduled Caste and Scheduled Tribe (1996-97 and 1997-98) Fourth Report, Vol. II, Rajasthan.

Kirit Singh (ed), Indian Development Report, Indira Gandhi Institute of Development Research, 1999-2000.

Scheduled Tribes Scheduled Area And Tribal Area in India, Government of India, 'Ministry of Social Justice And Empowerment' (Tribal Development Division), New Delhi.

World Development Report, 1999-2000, Oxford University Press.

National Policy on Education, 1986.

R. Govind (Ed.) Indian Education Report, National Institute of Education Planning & united Nations Education Science and Cultural Organosation, Oxford University Press, New Delhi, 2000.

Madhura Swaminathan and Vikas Rawal, 'Primary Education for All', Edited by Kirit S. Parikh, *Indira Gandhi Institute of Development Research',* India Development Report, 1999-2000.